THE WAGES of WRITING:
Per Word, Per Piece, or Perhaps

The Wages of Writing:
PER WORD, PER PIECE, or PERHAPS

Paul William Kingston and Jonathan R. Cole

Columbia University Press   New York   1986

This book is based on a final report entitled *Economic Survey of American Authors*, which was prepared by the Center for the Social Sciences of Columbia University for the Authors Guild Foundation, Inc.

Columbia University Press
New York   Guildford, Surrey
Copyright © 1986 Authors Guild Foundation, Inc.
All rights reserved

Printed in the United States of America

Library of Congress Cataloging-in-Publication Data

Kingston, Paul W.
The wages of writing.

Bibliography: p.
Includes index.
1. Authorship—Economic aspects—United States.
2. Authors, American—Economic conditions. 3. Authors, American—Social conditions. I. Cole, Jonathan R.
II. Title.
PN151.K45   1986   305'.98'0973   85-25543
ISBN 0-231-05786-5 (alk. paper)

This book is Smyth-sewn and printed on permanent and durable acid-free paper.

To our families:
Jane, Paul Brendan, and Ann
Joanna, Daniel, and Nonnie

Contents

Acknowledgments	ix
1. Introduction	1
Who Is an Author?	2
Headline Findings	4
A Historical Note	9
An Odd Case for the Sociology of Occupations	19
Plan of the Book	21
2. Description of the Survey of American Authors	23
Population Parameters: Unknown	23
Sampling Frames	25
Response	30
The Questionnaire	37
3. The Writing Occupation	41
Levels of Work Commitment	42
A Typology of Authors	44
Full-Timers: The On-and-Off Career	46
Part-Time Authors: Their Occupations	48
Attitudes Toward the Mixed Career	50
4. Income	55

Writing Income	56
Occupational Commitment and Income	64
Personal Characteristics, Writing Careers, and Earnings	70
Success Within Occupational Groups: Authorship as an Unusual Case	92
Total Personal and Family Income	99
Changes in Authors' Incomes	105
A Concluding Perspective	108

5. Social and Professional Connections Among Authors — 109

Professional Relationships with Other Authors	111
Work Relationships with Nonauthors	119
Writing: Individualistic Work	121
Sociable Contacts with Peers	123
The Social-Professional Connection	128
Patterns of Influence	133
Literary Life and the Sociology of Culture	136

6. Selected Portraits — 149

The Low-Income Writers	150
The Modestly Successful	152
The Best-Sellers	154
The Young	156
The Older Writers	157
Women Authors	158

Coda	163
Appendix A: Reproductions of the Questionnaires and Accompanying Cover Letters	167
Appendix B: Further Technical Considerations	183
Appendix C: Results from Multiple Regression Analyses	189
Appendix D: Classification of Awards and Publishing Houses	191
Notes	193
References	201
Index	205

Acknowledgments

IN ASSESSING the economic condition of American authors, our principal concern was to represent accurately the circumstances of this large and enormously disparate group. For this reason, our most immediate debt is to the 2,241 authors who took the time to complete the detailed questionnaire on which this book is based.

A large sample survey offers the only practicable way of obtaining systematic understanding of the economic condition of authors in general as well as the conditions of various types of authors. Properly constructed, it allows us to report on what is both common and uncommon within the ranks of authors. Of course, no amount of statistical artifice can create the "typical author." And, to be sure, individual circumstances and important nuances are inevitably lost in the aggregation of survey results. Yet the cooperation of these respondents allows us to move beyond impressions and speculations and present solid evidence about this little understood group.

As partial recompense for our debt to these authors, we can only hope that we met the charge of the Authors Guild Foundation, Inc., the financial sponsor of the study. In a cover letter to the authors in our sample, Peter Prescott, then president of the Authors Guild, wrote:

We hope to correct whatever distorted ideas people may have

about writers' incomes. Authors themselves, many of them, have only a limited perspective on the careers of others in their own profession. We expect that the study will provide an accurate up-to-date body of fact.

Indeed, our debt extends very directly to the Authors Guild Foundation, Inc. Officers of this organization not only initiated the idea for the project but committed funds to carry it out. Moreover, throughout the project, officers and staff at the Authors Guild were very cooperative. We owe special thanks to Bruce Bliven, John Brooks, Peter Heggie, Irwin Karp, and Sidney Offit—all members of an advisory board which was particularly helpful in constructing the questionnaire and arranging for in-depth interviews to complement the survey results.

The study was conducted at the Center for the Social Sciences, Columbia University. Madeline Simonson, Sally Otos, and Harry Saint Preux provided very capable, patient assistance in typing many drafts and handling a myriad of administrative and clerical tasks. Pnina Grinberg, Associate Director of the Center, provided us with extraordinary assistance throughout the project's duration. We gratefully acknowledge the help of the following Columbia College students who handled so many of the mundane yet crucial tasks associated with carrying out a survey: Yosef Francus, Michael Lamble, Thomas Nevitt, Robert Pash, and George Stephanopolous.

Harriet Zuckerman of Columbia's Department of Sociology and our colleague at the Center deserves our appreciation both for her substantive contributions to the analysis and for her helpful editorial advice.

Special mention is required of the guidance provided throughout the project by Robert K. Merton. He was our initial link to the Authors Guild Foundation. He worked tirelessly with us on the final report that was sent on to the foundation at the completion of the project. Those who work with Merton know of his unique ability to clarify concepts and to insist upon clear and precise language. He has been exceptionally generous with his time and help through all phases of the project.

We are also grateful to Ed Koren for permission to reproduce the cartoon frontispiece, which originally appeared in *Newsweek*, June 22, 1981, p. 77.

Acknowledgments

Beyond providing the necessary professional support, the Center also contributed financial assistance to the project. Because of the importance of the issue and the limited resources at the sponsoring agency, the Center committed itself to absorbing some costs of the project. Some forty-five years ago, the Bureau of Applied Social Research, which is the organizational precursor to the Center, embarked on a program of research focusing on mass communications. Studies ranged from "Daytime Serials: Their Audience and Their Effect on Buying" to "The Audience for the Voice of America in Norway." There was, then, a Bureau tradition of studies of the mass media and communications. With the publication of this book we hope to signal a renewed interest at the Center for the Social Sciences in the important study of the arts and in forms of communications.

Finally, the authors of this work on authors thank their families—Joanna, Daniel, and Nonnie, and Jane, Paul Brendan, and Ann for their support while this project was carried out.

'You can't ask a muse to live on $4.90 an hour'

There is no doubt about it, in the twentieth century if you are to come to be writing really writing you cannot make a living at it no not by writing. It was done in the nineteenth century but not in the eighteenth or in the twentieth no not possibly. And that is very curious, not so curious really but still very curious. In the eighteenth century not enough read to make any one earn their living and in the twentieth century too many read for any one to make their living by writing, the nineteenth century was just right it was in between.
Too few is as many as too many.
The end of the nineteenth century already they could not make a living writing.

Gertrude Stein, *Everybody's Autobiography*

1.
Introduction

> Almost anyone can be an author;
> the business is to collect money and fame
> from this state of being.
> A.A. Milne

> I love being a writer.
> What I can't stand is the paperwork.
> Peter De Vries

ROBERT BENCHLEY ONCE defined a freelance writer as "one who gets paid per word, per piece, or perhaps." As perfect as this definition is, we spoil it by asking: How much per word, or per piece?—and how often? This book addresses these questions. It is primarily about one part of the lives of American authors: their economic circumstances. In the public mind, the prevailing stereotypes of this condition appear to consist of contradictory images. One version is of the writer living in a cluttered garret working away on manuscripts, living in relative poverty. A contrasting image is of the author as the well-rewarded "talent," an image no doubt fostered by blockbuster contracts for paperback and movie rights. Such is the nature of stereotypes, of course, that one can find some measure of truth in both these images.

But, whatever their accuracy, these economic images have emerged in the absence of any systematic information. No reliable information has existed until now on how much authors earn from their writing, nor is any more known about their overall economic condition or their careers. Authors are much discussed and often publicly visible, but, curiously enough, the economic lives of these key figures in our culture have been much more a subject of speculation and anecdotal observation than rigorous study.

Surveys of public opinion have repeatedly found that the occupation of author is held in comparatively high regard by the American public. In terms of prestige, authors rank among the top 10 percent of all occupations (Reiss et al. 1961). The prestige of an occupation is generally positively associated with the typical income derived from it (Blau and Duncan 1967; Featherman and Hauser 1978; Treiman 1977); but whether the income of authors matches the lofty esteem in which they are held or whether they are a deviant case could only be a matter for conjecture.

Our central concern is to document the economic condition of authors, to provide a systematic corrective to some of the distorted views that may exist. The study is based on a large-scale sample survey of American authors carried out in 1980. With the cooperation of 2,241 authors who responded to the survey, we have obtained the necessary data for reasonably reliable estimates—at any rate, the best estimates yet available—of the economic circumstances of American authors. This survey of authors is unmatched in important respects: its large number of respondents, its intention to represent the full population of book writers in America; and the breadth of its substantive concerns. With this large number of respondents, we are able to report on the economic conditions of authors in general, as well as on the economic conditions of various types of authors, a group which proves difficult even to define.

Who Is an Author? Definition of the Population

From the outset we faced a difficult and complex question: who is the author? Any single definition is bound to raise objections. Some time

Introduction

ago, for example, Malcolm Cowley took a broad view in defining a writer as "a man or woman who writes." Yet this does not help much to define an author for the purposes of a systematic survey. Does being an author involve a certain minimum commitment of time and energies? Is self-definition enough, or must a person be published, published within recent years, or even earn a certain amount of money to qualify?

We do not attempt to offer a definitive answer. Instead, we take as inclusive an approach as possible in defining the population of the survey. We consider the population to be *all contemporary American writers who have had at least one book published*, without imposing further criteria.[1] Such flexibility seemed especially desirable as we approached a group that is so diverse and difficult to define clearly without being arbitrary.

To be sure, a priori definitions involving time commitments to writing, percentage contribution of writing earnings to family incomes, recentness of publication, and the like could have been devised. However, by including all living book writers in our population, such matters may be treated as variables. To illustrate this point, the population might have been defined as currently active authors—that is, writers who have had a book published within, say, the last three years. For some purposes this definition may be very reasonable, but it excludes many slow writers or intermittent writers from consideration. With our inclusive approach, though, recentness of publication can be related to the economic returns of writing. Recently published authors can then be studied as a potentially interesting subsample and can be compared with writers who have not published books recently.

We should point out, however, that even this broad definition excludes some who may have a reasonable claim to being considered an author. Our definition means that every member of the population must have had at least one success in convincing some publisher to produce his or her book. The men and women who produce a manuscript only to have it sit in a desk drawer without publication may keenly aspire to be published book writers, and indeed may have the talent of many who have had their work published. Yet, however promising or deserving these unpublished writers may be, they are not included in the population of this study. If, as is widely believed, young writers are having an increasingly difficult time becoming published, then we are missing a full perspective on a group whose fate will surely affect the future state of American writing.

The focus on book writers is also somewhat restrictive and may appear partially arbitrary. After all, writers of articles and other short pieces also communicate with the written word. In a relatively brief space, they offer similar possibilities of entertainment, information, and stimulation. Undoubtedly, articles, essays, and short stories contribute to the richness and diversity of American writing, and the writers of these pieces deserve consideration. Still, very few writers (other than academics in some fields) commit themselves solely to such efforts. Let us further note that writers primarily committed to articles who have also published a book are included within our population.

So it is the diverse group of contemporary American authors who have published at least one book that we seek to analyze—their economic condition, their occupational pursuits, their social and professional connections. Collecting the necessary data for this analysis involved unusual difficulties in defining the population and obtaining information from a representative sample. The difficulties involved in both tasks should not be underestimated and, inevitably, they are not fully resolved—or even resolvable.

Suffice it to say, we feel reasonably confident that the findings of this survey accurately portray the economic situation of American authors. This conclusion is based on technical analyses reported in detail in chapter 2 where we discuss sample selection, data collection procedures, and survey response (including several checks on possible response bias). A copy of the questionnaire which is the primary source of data for our study is presented in appendix A.

Headline Findings

Before detailing the particulars of the economic condition of American authors, we highlight below some of the headline findings. Accompa-

Introduction

nying stories and analytical sidepieces document and extend these findings in the ensuing chapters.

INCOME FROM WRITING. Most authors cannot make ends meet from their writing alone.

- For the year 1979, the representative (i.e., median) author in the survey earned a total of $4,775 from writing; that is, 50 percent earned less than this amount. (This dollar figure represents total income derived from book royalties, magazine and newspaper articles, motion picture and television work, and so on.)
- A quarter of the authors earned less than $1,000 from their writing; 10 percent of the authors had a writing income of more than $45,000; 5 percent, more than $80,000.
- For authors without any other regular paid position, the median writing income was $7,500; for part-time authors, $2,600.
- The representative author had an hourly writing income of $4.90.
- The representative author (as indicated by the median) received 98 cents of every writing dollar from books, including both royalty payments and subsidiary rights; the remaining two cents came from articles and scripts. Royalty payments alone typically accounted for 87 cents of every dollar.
- About half of the recently published authors (1977–1980) within each writing genre—with the lone exception of genre fiction writers—earned less than $5,000 in 1979 from writing.
- Authors' income from writing is subject to sharp short-time fluctuations; in 1979, 5 percent of the authors earned about ten times as much from their writing as in the year before, while another 5 percent earned only one-fifth as much as the year before.
- A quarter of the authors earned five times as much from writing in their best year as in 1979, and 10 percent

earned fully fifteen times as much in their best year as in 1979.

TOTAL PERSONAL AND FAMILY INCOMES. Although the vast majority of authors cannot make ends meet from their writing, their total personal and family incomes typically far exceed their incomes from writing, either because of income from other work or their spouse's support.

- Authors reported median *personal* incomes from all sources of $27,000 in 1979. (Personal income represents the total of writing income, professional payments, salaries, and income from investments—including those jointly held with a spouse—pensions, and Social Security.)
- The total 1979 personal income of 25 percent of the authors was less than $13,000, while another 25 percent received more than $45,000. The lowest 10 percent received less than $5,000, the highest 10 percent, almost $80,000.
- Part-time authors that same year had a median personal income of $30,000 compared to roughly $20,000 for full-time authors.
- The median total *family* income for all authors was $38,000. (Family income represents the total of personal income and spouse's personal income, including income from investments separately held; for the unmarried, personal and family income are the same.)
- The total family incomes of authors varied substantially. The top quarter of authors had family incomes totaling $60,000 or more; the lowest quarter, $23,000. At the very extremes, the lowest tenth received only $12,000 and the highest tenth as much as $100,000.
- Half of the authors had spouses in the labor force. The large gap between total personal and total family income reflected the contributions of spouses. Authors' husbands had median incomes of some $26,000; authors' wives had median incomes of just under $4,000.

Introduction

THE WRITING OCCUPATION. Analyses of the financial return from writing must take into account the great diversity of the economic lives of authors.

- Forty-six percent of the authors held a regular paid position besides freelance writing.
- Most of the other jobs held by authors were in the professional occupations.
- The representative author (as indicated by the median) devoted twenty hours a week to actual writing or work directly related to a book or article. Thirty-four percent of authors without another job spent forty or more hours a week writing; 28 percent of those with another job wrote less than ten hours a week.
- The mixed occupational career of many part-time authors was apparently a matter of economic pressure rather than preference. Forty-six percent of the part-time authors expressed a definite willingness to drop their other work if they could match their present total income by writing full time; another 22 percent thought that they would "possibly" like to make such a change.
- The large majority of part-time authors found writing more satisfying than their other jobs.

WRITING INCOME AND CHARACTERISTICS OF AUTHORS AND THEIR WORK.

- Prolific authors, of course, earned more than others. Forty-three percent of the authors with no more than two published books to their credit earned less than $2,500 from writing in 1979, in contrast to the 12 percent of authors who had published at least ten books.
- Genre fiction was the most lucrative kind of writing: a fifth of genre fiction authors earned at least $50,000 in 1979, almost three times the rate of adult nonfiction writers.
- Winners of honorific awards for their writing earned a little more than authors who had not received such

recognition. Among the prizewinners writing income remained unrelated to prestige of the award.
- The median income of male authors (60 percent of those in the sample) was $5,000 in 1979; for female authors, $4,000. Thirty-seven percent of the men and 40 percent of the women earned less than $2,500; 11 percent of the men and 6 percent of the women earned more than $50,000 from writing.
- Considered together, black, Hispanic, and Asian authors did not have significantly different writing incomes from white authors.
- Where authors lived had little to do with how much they earned from writing: 44 percent of New York–based writers earned less than $5,000 from writing in 1979 compared to 51 percent based in California and 52 percent based in the South. Nor were New Yorkers more apt than authors located in other regions to earn upward of $50,000.
- The financial fate of writers was not affected by their social class origins; incomes are much alike among those coming from white-collar and blue-collar families.
- College graduates fared no better, on the average, than authors with less formal education. Among the graduates, the prestige of the colleges attended had no discernible effect on subsequent writing-related income.

SOCIAL AND PROFESSIONAL CONNECTIONS.

- Thirty percent of all authors met socially with other authors at least once a month; the rest, only "every few months" or "rarely."
- A fifth of all authors "always" or "usually" discussed ideas for books or work in progress with other authors; the rest "sometimes" or "never" did.

- About a fifth of all authors counted no fellow authors as a "good friend"; three-fifths had three or fewer "good friends" who are authors.

A Historical Note on Authorship as a Profession

While such are the conditions of contemporary authors, they are obviously rooted in the occupational fates of their predecessors. Today, when there is a trend toward professionalizing everything, it might appear that men and women of letters belong to an ancient profession. Yet, in fact, authorship, at least as an independent occupation divorced from the courts and patronage systems, has relatively recent origins in the late seventeenth and early eighteenth centuries in England. It does not appear as a profession in the United States until the first decades of the nineteenth century.

The causes for the emerging independence of authors have themselves become a subject for authors.[2] In this section, we discuss briefly several of the most prominent causes, while keeping to our major theme: how did authors earn their living during this early period, and how much money were they apt to earn?

Although minor disagreements exist about when the fundamental change in the status of authors occurred, Beljame, Bonham-Carter, Collins, and Watt, among other scholars, trace the origins of profound shifts in the profession to the period in England following the Revolution of 1688. Beljame attributes the most significant changes to Addison's development of *The Spectator* around 1710; others identify the transformation with somewhat earlier social changes. All these scholars agree on at least several points. First, fundamental shifts took place in the latter part of the seventeenth and early eighteenth centuries in England which led to greater independence of authors and the beginnings of authorship as a true profession; second, after these changes, authors were no longer strictly dependent upon the patronage of the rich and powerful, and could rely increasingly on an emerging public audience for their works (Dobrée in Beljame 1948; Coser 1965; Collins 1927, 1928); and third, the processes of change in the status of authors were sociologically complex and cannot be identified with any single cause.

In this connection Victor Bonham-Carter notes:

> Dryden's death in 1700 is a convenient landmark, for the 18th—not the 17th—century was the watershed of professional writing from the business point of view. In short the 1700's witnessed the progressive replacement of personal by public patronage, i.e. by earnings from commercial publications—the change partly due to the Copyright Act of 1709 which... gave the author limited legal protection—but due also to the initiative of certain authors who followed Dryden and set a vital precedent for the future: among them, Richardson, Fielding, and others already considered. (1978:22)

Dryden set an example, of course, by the excellent terms that he obtained (£1,200) for his edition of Virgil. Nonetheless, it is clear that even in Dryden's time authors were most frequently in the position of humiliating dependence upon their patrons. They simply did not enjoy financial independence.

The income which he drew from his writings was small and precarious, and it was this problem of a livelihood which placed him so completely at the mercy of a frivolous society and its capricious leaders. The rewards which a professional writer might hope for were of three kinds:
1. Profit from the theater.
2. Sale of his works to booksellers.
3. Gifts.

All three were... very modest and most uncertain. (Beljame 1948: 106–108)

Indeed, from theatrical performances the best that a playwright of 1700 could hope for was the profit on the third performance. And many a play never made it that far. Even if the author enjoyed such "success," he was most often responsible for the sale of tickets and the gathering of his patrons and friends to contribute to his welfare.

A stark contrast can be drawn between the financial fates of Milton and Pope. Milton, by virtue of an agreement dated April 27, 1667, received the grand sum of £5 for the first impression of 1,300

Introduction

copies of *Paradise Lost*; it was not increased even a shilling for the second and third impressions. Pope, who had received but £7 for the *Rape of the Lock* and £32 5s. for *Windsor Forest* early in his career, had the later good fortune of receiving the then incredible sum of approximately £9,000 through the sale of subscriptions after 1715 for his translations of the *Iliad* and the *Odyssey* (Bonham-Carter 1978:23). Of course, the independence achieved by Pope was by no means typical of this period, but it did signal the beginning of the possibility for authors to receive substantial returns for their work.

Indeed, even in this earliest period of independence, we can chart wide variations in authors' incomes. There were a few authors in the early eighteenth century who received the equivalent of blockbuster contracts, or who managed through their personal initiative and the work of several publishers, such as Tonson or Lintot, to obtain hefty returns for their works. The vast majority of writers, however, made up the inhabitants of the famous Grub Street. Lewis Coser remarks on its composition:

> To be sure, a majority of the Grub Street hacks simply had no talent and would have had no chance to become independent men of letters under any conditions. But Grub Street consisted not only of the dregs of the writing profession; many major writers also served long sentences there before receiving due recognition. Some of them became the victims of a system in which the bookseller wielded a very heavy hand over the author. (Coser 1965:43)

In the eighteenth century the book trade was still far too small to be able to provide significant rewards for a substantial number of authors. In discussing the situation in Grub Street, Bonham-Carter notes:

> Sheer poverty compelled many of them to sell their souls to whomever would give them work—for political pamphlets, scandal sheets, pornography, the grind of ghosting and devilling, or any of the other chores associated with starvation scribbling. And it was poverty that gained them a reputation for minor crookery and evil living, cheating tradesmen, haunting whorehouses and drink shops, and dodging bailiffs and landlords. They were not alone. Grub Street had its rogues on both sides of the fence: authors such as Tom Brown and the brilliant Richard Savage (Samuel

Johnson's friend); and publishers like Abel Roper and Edmund Currll (who was said to lodge his hacks three in a bed), who became a byword for piracy and scurrility. (1978:28)

Watt has pointed out, however, that in one sense Grub Street's unfavorable image was a myth. Booksellers supported more authors at higher wages than had the older patronage system (Watt 1957:54). The ultimate meaning of Grub Street was that it represented the market economy's infiltration into the literary profession. With the application of market mechanisms of supply and demand, authors altered the type of works that they produced. The market favored certain genres over others—for example, prose over poetry. And the new economic structure provided rewards for speed and prolixity more than for parsimony and verbal grace.

One of the causes for this emerging independence of authors after the Revolution of 1688 was linked to politics. Writers began to work for politicians and ministers who were gaining ascendency in the House of Commons. They became valuable commodities, who were sought after by many political figures. With increased demand for their services came increased security and increased esteem, at least for a minority of authors. Beljame notes this link between economics and prestige:

Their profession rose in public estimation. As soon as it was clear that literature might be the road to wealth and dignity, it was no longer scorned and looked down upon. . . . Hitherto, literature had seemed—not unjustifiably—a career which led only to endless disillusionment, if not irretrievable misery. The luckless Wight who was trying to live by his pen met only with contempt—tempered, in exceptional cases only, by the respect which talent commands. . . . The moment that the author became eligible for high employment and fat salaries, he was looked on with another eye and granted what he had never enjoyed before: respect and esteem. Writing was no longer a trade but a career—a career leading to riches and honor; and this new respect for literature inspired a new attitude to authors. They no longer formed a class apart, they were received in high society not as proteges but on terms of full equality with the greatest. (Beljame 1978: 219–220)

The rise of authorship as a profession has also been

Introduction

attributed to the significant growth of a reading public. As Coser notes:

> The social ascent of the middle class brought the emergence of new strata with enough leisure and education to develop a taste for reading books. In the preceding century this taste was limited to a relatively small elite. In the 17th century, the bulk of the middle class, if they read at all, read mainly religious tracts and political broadsheets. Only in the 18th century did the growing middle class broaden their concerns and evince wider interest in other types of literature. (Coser 1965:38)

Indeed, the general rise in standard of living in the eighteenth century brought increased leisure activity to middle-class homes, and reading was among the most popular. In part, the conditions for reading were brought about by the increased size of such homes; in the seventeenth century, they had afforded little privacy and required people to spend much of their leisure time at local taverns, coffee houses, plays, and operas. By the eighteenth century, the increase in wealth was reflected in more spacious living quarters, which enabled members of the family to read in relative privacy (Coser 1965:41).

A related cause for the improved standing of authors was the new role that women played as readers of fiction and magazines. Reflecting the prevailing attitudes toward women and the consequences of those attitudes, Addision wrote in 1713:

> There are some reasons why learning is more adapted to the female world than to the male. As in the first place, because they have more spare time on their hands, and lead a more sedentary life... There is another reason why those especially who are women of quality, should apply themselves to letters, namely because their husbands are generally strangers to them. (Quoted in Watt 1957:43–44).

In fact, middle-class women were more apt than their male counterparts to take enjoyment in the quiet relaxation of reading. Women read Richardson, Fielding, Smollett, and Goldsmith, among others, for moral guidance as well as for relaxation.

Among the middle-class readers, women outnumbered men. While the middle-class man was involved in business or trade, the middle-class woman managed the sphere of consumption. To her fell the duty of evolving styles of conduct appropriate to the new status her family had achieved. She was helped in this task by the leads provided by the new middle-class literature. (Coser 1965:40)

Even though there was a substantial growth in the potential audience of writers, that growth must be kept in perspective. The book trade in the eighteenth century was still highly constrained by two factors: the low level of literacy in England and the cost of purchasing books. While good estimates of the size of the reading public do not exist, the best available suggest that the number did not exceed 80,000 in the 1690s in a population which exceeded six million, that is, only about 1 percent. Data on the circulation of weekly newspapers around 1700 show a figure of about 44,000; and for a daily in 1753, the figure was 23,673 (Collins 1928:29; Watt 1957:36). Thus, if England was, as Johnson said, "a nation of readers," he must have been referring to growth that occurred after 1750 or to the relative size of the reading public.

The economics of book publishing represented another major impediment to the sale of books and consequently the incomes of authors. Ian Watt, in discussing the rise of the novel, indicates that "the price of a novel... would feed a family for a week or two" (p. 42). The cost of *Tom Jones*, for instance, exceeded the laborer's average weekly wage. Of course, less expensive forms of literary entertainment existed. But the limited size of the public able to afford novels was surely a factor influencing the foci of authors' attention—leading them to write in genres that would have some prospect for sale.

Even so, the growth of the publishing industry itself, along with certain changes in marketing arrangements, contributed to the rise of authorship as an independent profession. With the development of booksellers (i.e., publishers) in the eighteenth century came a set of complex relationships between author and publisher. The relationship then between author and publisher was not dramatically different from that of today—structurally induced ambivalence. Booksellers of the early eighteenth century developed a variety of techniques for increasing the size of the audience for their products. The most important among these was the development of advance subscriptions,

Introduction

a method by which publishers reduced the risk associated with publishing by obtaining guarantees of reasonable sales before actual publication. It was often the task of authors to secure subscribers, and indeed authors sometimes acted as door-to-door salesmen in their attempts to find subscriptions for their volumes. Dryden's *Virgil* and Pope's *Iliad* were published by subscription and in fact returned such handsome sums that Pope by the age of thirty five had become rich and independent (Beljame 1948:369; Coser 1965:42–43).

Throughout the eighteenth century, at least after the Copyright Act of 1709, the principal source of income for authors was through the sale of copyrights. However, several variations in the form of publication were adopted to varying degrees during this period. Other than the sale of copyright, these included profit sharing, commission publication, and subscription (Bonham-Carter 1978:25). For example, in the latter part of the eighteenth century, Adam Smith arranged with Hume's friend Strahan to divide the profits from various editions of the *Wealth of Nations* (1776). Strahan bought the copyright for the first edition and divided profits from subsequent editions with Smith. Similarly, Strahan and Edward Gibbon struck a deal for the profits from *The Decline and Fall* (1776), by which Gibbon was to receive two-thirds of the proceeds from the first volume. The profit sharing form of publication was one which typically triggered the latent ambivalence in the publisher-author relationship. Authors contended that publishers frequently inflated the costs of production to lower the disclosed profit.

Commission publishing, "whereby the author himself or a benefactor pays for the cost of production," represented another form of publication (Bonham-Carter 1978:26). Apparently this form was never particularly popular among authors or booksellers. Authors were convinced that booksellers would not push their books in order to obtain copyrights at a minimal cost. Publishing houses were not enamored of this adaptation because of the small incentives for sales.

Subscription was a widely adopted format. A royalty system similar to that which predominates today (where authors and publishers agree upon a royalty set at some percentage of the book's retail price, with possible escalating percentages from increased sales) simply was irrelevant to the authors of the eighteenth century, and did not come into general practice until the beginning of the twentieth century.

Even with these innovations, the simple fact remains, that in eighteenth century Britain, the vast majority of authors could not survive exclusively on their writing-related income.

Outside Grub Street and the higher haunts of journalism, where few men of letters such as Hazlitt, Southey, and Leigh Hunt, did manage to subsist more or less on their writing, the majority of authors had to insure a livelihood by combining authorship with other forms of employment, or by reliance on private means, or sometimes both: as in the case of Wordsworth, who held the post of 'Distributor of Stamps for the County of Westmoreland' 1813-42, or John Keats—for a short time a hospital dresser, an unpaid apothecary, but who finally fell back on friends and family money. (Bonham-Carter 1978:44)

So it was in the Britain of the eighteenth and nineteenth centuries, and so it is today in the United States, as we shall see.

If the turning point for authorship as a profession occurred in England in the beginning of the eighteenth century, in America it did not occur until at least a century later. The American experience with professional authorship did not really reach a take-off stage until the first quarter of the nineteenth century. Although gothic adventures produced in England and written principally by women working in anonymous secrecy were imported to America, there was no fortune to be made in that business. Most women authors during this period received a small flat fee—somewhere between five and twenty guineas per book. As William Charvat points out, it was not until Cooper's success in the early 1820s that we could claim to have one single American novelist who was financially successful (1968:20).[3] In fact, he dates the profession of authorship in the United States to the 1820s when James Fenimore Cooper and Washington Irving discovered that readers were willing to buy their books on a regular basis.

Charvat points to three key factors that transformed the occupation of writing into one which was more profitable. For one, authors began to write on diverse subjects of general interest. This broke down formal barriers between reading groups, and books began

Introduction

to appeal to a wider audience among those who were literate. For another, an increasing number of people were able and willing to pay for books; others could get them through a growing number of circulating libraries.[4] Finally, authors were helped by the astuteness, entrepreneurial spirit, and increasing business experience among publishers, who began to forge a closer linkage between authors and their readers (1968:30). While these factors improved the economic condition of authors, they were themselves dependent on the ability of authors to produce manuscripts in a timely fashion and on the increased prestige of authorship within the society.

What were the actual incomes of American authors during the middle half of the nineteenth century? As noted, until the 1820s no American novelist was financially successful. Toward midcentury the pattern that we observe today held for most men and women of letters. The vast majority of active authors, many of whom had significant reputations, worked only part time at writing. Most of these writers could not make ends meet on writing-related income. In order for them to pursue their writing interests, they had to hold second jobs. In fact, by midcentury there were probably more part-time, or what we have called the "intermittent full-time," authors than there were writers devoting themselves exclusively to literary activities.

It was not unusual for prestigious writers to secure relatively lucrative positions through political patronage. Hawthorne's job at the Boston Custom-House, arranged by friends, is a case in point.[5] This position protected him from financial bad weather for quite some time. Hawthorne notes, however, in "The Custom-House," which appears as an introduction to the second edition of *The Scarlet Letter*, that few of his colleagues at the custom-house even knew of his work, and if they did, they could not have been less interested:

> None of them, I presume, had ever read a page of my inditing, or would have cared a fig the more for me, if they had read them all; nor would have mended the matter, in the least, had those same unprofitable pages been written with a pen like that of Burns or of Chaucer, each of whom was a Custom-House officer in his day, as well as I. It is a good lesson—though it may often be a hard one—for a man who has dreamed of literary fame, and of making for himself a rank among the world's dignitaries by such means, to step aside out of the narrow circle in which

his claims are recognized, and to find how utterly devoid of significance, beyond that circle, is all that he achieves, and all he aims at.

Other notable nineteenth-century authors who had a difficult time of it included Thoreau, who lived from hand to mouth and apparently did not mind, and Emerson who wrote in 1838 that he owned a house, $22,000 worth of stocks earning 6%, and an income from lectures varying from $400 to $800 a year (Charvat 1968:58). Even though some novelists began to live off their writing by the 1820s, it was not until after the Civil War that a single American poet could live comfortably with income derived from writing.

At the time of his death in 1891, Melville left an estate worth $13,261.31 (pp. 191–203). Melville's will shows that he had about $4,500 in cash, another $8,000 in U.S. registered bonds, and $600 worth of personal books, which numbered roughly 1,000 volumes. After expenses, the net value of the estate then came to approximately $12,000.

The total income that Melville derived from English and American sales of his first five books as well as the English sale of his sixth, *Moby Dick*, was approximately $8,000, amounting to roughly $1,600 a year for five years, but his liabilities exceeded assets for this period. For the period 1860 to 1868, Melville was practically without any income whatsoever from his novels, magazine publications, or lectures. During these years he heavily relied on income generated from his father-in-law's estate, though it was not sufficient to support a household with four children. A second job became essential. In 1866, Melville began working as Inspector of Customs in the District of New York at a salary of $4.00 a day, that is, approximately $1,250 a year. This position was actually quite precarious since the New York Custom House, notorious for its corruption, was almost invariably under scrutiny for its well-known feather-bedding, and jobs were never secure.

What is perhaps most remarkable about the economic situation of literary figures in late eighteenth-and early nineteenth-century Britain and America is how similar it is to the current financial position of authors. Of course, much has changed. The size of the reading public, the proportion of the population that is literate, the number and types of books published, and the sheer number of people who are authors, have grown, if not exponentially, certainly at a very rapid rate. Nonetheless, it appears to be as true today as it was in the

18th century that few authors are capable of subsisting on writing-related income. To be sure, writing has been freed from a system of patronage, and the profession of authorship is one which carries with it substantial prestige. But it remains a profession which does not reflect the normal correlation between income and esteem. While most highly respected occupations also yield substantial incomes, this is not the case with authorship. We can point to the occasional author who makes substantial sums of money from writing, whether it be an Alexander Pope in the eighteenth century or a Norman Mailer today. But for the vast majority, it remains either a low-paying occupation or only one of several occupations which support individual writers and their families.

An Odd Case for the Sociology of Occupations

Both our headlines about present-day conditions and the historical excursus plainly indicate that the occupation of author is odd in many ways. It neither provides a living wage to the overwhelming number who meet the condition of having published at least one book (though some do spectacularly well), nor imposes a distinctive, common pattern of work activity on those who labor in the occupation. For the most part, our concern is to delineate certain characteristics of this diverse group as a whole, as well as to provide a detailed descriptive account of specific types of authors.

Yet while authors are interesting in their own right, we also consider the occupation of author as an instructive case for the sociology of occupations. It is instructive precisely because it is so differentiated and unstructured—an occupation which Theodore Caplow's standard volume has described as one of those "occupational groups so vague as to defy precise definition" (1954:63). Even in late twentieth century America, where we are experiencing what William J. Goode has called "the professionalization of everything," it remains unclear whether the occupation of writer or author can be correctly classified among the professions. Bernard Barber, among many others, has noted that the hallmark of a professional is specialized knowledge and authority to use that knowledge within a specific context. But would authors qualify as professionals using such definitions? As a "deviant case," the analytical significance of an occupation such as author derives from the comparative perspective which it provides.

For instance, as factors related to status attainment (especially as indicated by occupation) have become better understood, there has been an emerging concern to understand patterns of success *within* occupations; but to date these analyses have tended to focus on comparatively structured occupations. Thus, to the extent that economic differentiation within the ranks of authors is, or is not, accounted for by factors which are of consequence within other occupations, analysis of this unusual profession can complement existing research on intraoccupational attainment. We can then raise in a broader light a theoretical question: what is it about the structure of various occupations which determines the kind and extent of social patterning of economic success? Indeed, we are led to turn from the descriptive material of the case to a consideration of this and other theoretical issues in the sociology of occupations.

SOCIAL AND PROFESSIONAL CONNECTIONS

Besides considering the economic returns of writing, we also look to another little-studied dimension of the work lives of authors—the social and professional connections among them. Again, the public seems to hold conflicting views of authors. Coexisting with the image of the isolate, the recluse typing away in seclusion, speaking to the world only through the written word, is the image of the public figure, sometimes a social lion, engaged in intellectual circles, interacting with fellow authors and others by dint of personality as well as writing product. Of course, the fact that examples of each tendency can be readily cited—Salinger and Mailer perhaps being the most noted exemplars—indicates that neither image wholly reflects the truth.

Nonetheless, among informed observers it is a common view, prominently emphasized in Lewis Coser, Charles Kadushin, and

Introduction

Walter Powell's recent work, *Books: The Culture and Commerce of Publishing*, that American intellectual life is diffuse, only weakly reinforced by personal networks among authors. It is largely an open matter whether the famous intellectual-literary circles ever encompassed more than a small number of the authors of their times. Yet the view that authors are now, by and large, a disconnected lot also rests on anecdotal observation, not systematic analysis.

Our survey provides material that allows us to document—with a broad brush, to be sure—the kinds of interactions authors have with each other. We look at the extent of their professional assistance to one another. As the headlines indicated, authors seem neither very sociable nor very collegial with their professional counterparts. The sociology of occupations thus suggests that we have a deviant case on our hands in another respect. In analyzing the connections among authors, then, we can offer some theoretical perspective on the social organization of occupations in addition to new information on the social organization of our cultural life.

Plan of the Book

The details of our discussion of the economic condition of American authors are organized as follows:

In chapter 2 we discuss the Columbia Survey of American Authors, the source of data for this study. Since the ability to generalize to the population of authors rests on the representativeness of the sample, we urge readers to refer to this technical material. Not all readers, we recognize, are inclined to such discussions; and to those who may prefer to go directly to the substantive material, let us simply say that our general confidence in the representativeness of the sample rests on extensive analyses.

In chapter 3 we focus on the widely varying commitments authors have to writing as an occupation. We create a typology of authors based on their commitment to writing as an economic activity. (This typology is central to our subsequent analysis of income in chapter 4.) We consider the authors' attitudes toward writing and their other jobs, if any.

In chapter 4 the incomes of authors are examined in two main respects: the economic return on their writing; their personal and family incomes. We analyze how economic success in writing is related to various personal characteristics of authors and to various contingencies in their writing careers. In effect, we attempt to detail how the economic success of authors is socially patterned. These results bear upon the question of what social factors influence economic success or failure within occupations.

The social linkage among authors, in both their writing and their social lives, is discussed in chapter 5. The central question of this chapter is to what extent and in what ways authors engage each other.

Chapter 6 presents six short statistical sketches of selected groups of authors: low-income writers, the modestly successful, authors of best-sellers, young authors, older writers, and women authors. We look at their occupational commitments, financial circumstances, and links to other authors.

Finally, in a brief coda, we allude to some of the limitations and implications of our survey-based assessment of the economic condition of American authors.

2.
Description of the Survey of American Authors

AS INDICATED in chapter 1, the population of the study is composed of all contemporary American writers of published books. Our survey attempts to represent the economic condition of this population. There is often a problematic linkage between the definition of a population and the representation of this population through sample-based survey research. As will be evident, the characteristics of our population posed unusual difficulties for survey research, and sampling from this population presented considerable problems. Beyond the sampling problem, we also achieved a response to the survey that is lower than optimal. While we believe that the results presented here offer a reasonably accurate portrait of the economic condition of American authors, the problems of population parameters, sampling, and response rates lead us to approach the results with caution.

Population Parameters: Unknown

Whatever their definition of author, researchers must inevitably face the problem that the characteristics of the general population of authors are virtually unknown. Census data are only of small help. The *Standard Occupational Classification Manual*, which is used by the Census Bureau in defining occupational titles, defines authors as follows:

This minor group [sic] includes occupations involving originating and editing written material for publication in printed form and for spoken use, broadcasting, and dramatic presentation; and translating or interpreting written or spoken words from one language to another.

This working definition of authors suffers from being at once overinclusive and underinclusive. It is overinclusive because it includes many occupations only loosely connected with writing rather than requiring actual writing, let alone publication. It is underinclusive in leaving out published writers who, having other jobs as well, happen not to designate their principal occupation as author when filling out the census form. Furthermore, no recognized official directory of writers exists, and all organizational membership lists are clearly incomplete with respect to any sensible definition of contemporary American authors.

The parameters of the population of authors, then, are largely a mystery. This is a particularly vexing problem. Not knowing the characteristics of a population, it becomes extremely difficult to draw a sample and impossible to ascertain its exact relationship to the larger population. Survey research is typically based on random samples drawn from well-defined populations with known attributes. Without such prior knowledge of the population's attributes, we can only draw tentative inferences from the results obtained from the sample. The paucity of knowledge about the author population does not mean that the results based on a sample are necessarily inaccurate. It does mean that if we had established knowledge about the author population and had a reliable census of American authors, we would be able to assess with great confidence the results secured from a sample which precisely reflects the entire population.

As it is, however, we face serious difficulties in drawing firm conclusions about the representativeness of our survey. We deal with this in part by providing some necessarily rather crude analyses of response bias, but our claim of having a representative sample essentially rests on the assumption that our large sampling frames include a representative though not exhaustive listing of authors as defined here. For this reason, the sampling frames must be described in detail. Nevertheless, because of the problems in obtaining parameters of the population of American authors, results reported here should be treated with caution.

Sampling Frames

Our inclusive strategy in defining the population as all published authors was, by necessity, consciously guided by the availability of lists which could serve as a basis for drawing a sample of authors. The lists we considered most suitable for a sampling frame consisted of individuals who had at least one published book to their credit. In short, for both analytical and practical reasons, we broadly defined the population in this way.

While we considered various possible sources as sampling frames, all had drawbacks—usually a combination of an obviously unrepresentative listing and practical limitations (such as lack of home addresses). As the sponsor of this study, however, the Authors Guild Foundation conveniently made the membership and invitee lists of the Authors Guild available. Of all practically usable sources, these lists represent the largest number of book writers.[1]

We sampled from two separate lists: the membership list of the Authors Guild as of fall 1979, and the guild's list of book writers who had been invited to join the guild within the past four years but had declined.

The Authors Guild Membership List. Almost 5,000 writers were members of the Authors Guild at the time of drawing the sample in 1979. Qualifications for membership in the guild are relatively undemanding:

By resolution of the Authors Guild Council, any author who shall have had a book published within seven years prior to his application; or any author who shall have three works, fiction or non-fiction, published by a magazine or magazines of general circulation within eighteen months prior to his application; or any author whose professional standing, in the opinion of the Membership Committee, shall entitle him to membership whether or not he shall have had work published as defined above, shall be eligible to join The Authors Guild as an active member with voting rights.

Every type of commercially published author, without regard for the putative quality of his or her work, is therefore qualified for membership.

Before sampling authors we were not able to identify writers among guild members who had never published a book. The staff at the guild told us that virtually every member had published at least one book; they could think of only a handful who had not. (The results of the survey confirm this: more than 99 percent of the sample had published one or more books.)

Moreover, the guild actively seeks new members across a wide range of writing genres. From reports in *Publishers Weekly* and in the *Library Journal*, the guild's staff continually draws up a list of authors to be invited to join the organization. They try to include most authors who write for a general audience and have not received an invitation in recent years. Academic and technically oriented writers, however, usually do not receive invitations because the staff has found that they are not very frequently inclined to join. Also, authors of several books are relatively likely to receive an invitation, though the guild attempts to invite every new novelist. While not fully inclusive, then, their invitation policy guarantees that writers seeking to appeal to a general audience know that they are welcome to join.

The Invitees' List. In the course of efforts to increase membership, the guild's staff keeps a list of all those who have been invited to join. Because it seemed possible that the guild members differed from writers who were not members, we decided to sample from this list as well.

Although this list of invitees goes back many years (with some duplications because of multiple invitations), we sampled only from those invited in the interval 1976–79. Authors on this list, therefore, had at least one book published since 1976. (This publication need not have been their first or only publication in these years.) We decided to sample only these four years because the likelihood of mistaken addresses in the years before seemed prohibitively high. Even so, we risked having considerable trouble in contacting respondents because many of the addresses were in care of their publishers, and forwarding addresses would have expired in many cases. The list of invitees for the years 1976–79 comprised some 3,750 names.

The Sampling Frames Together. Considered together, these two sampling frames made up a very large but indeterminate number of those meeting our inclusive definition of an author. Recall that the membership list is the largest of all organizations of writers, and the great number of authors who publish a book for a general audience are invited to join. The combined lists, however, still exclude or at least undercount two groups of authors: authors of academically and technically oriented books; authors who had been invited to join the guild before 1976 and had not received another invitation since that time.[2] These exclusions cannot be ignored in evaluating the suitability of the sampling frames. And yet, we believe, any biases introduced by these exclusions are not likely to distort seriously the subsequent analysis—or at least do not bias upward our estimates of the financial rewards derived directly from writing.

We expect that authors of academic and technical books, with a few exceptions among textbook authors, do not generally earn much from their writing. If they were included in greater numbers in the sample, estimates of the writing income of authors would likely decline to some degree. Of course, many of these writers do not expect to earn much from their writing. For academics in particular, a primary motivation for publication is professional recognition in itself, and thus their financial return from writing is somewhat tangential to an analysis of the economic conditions of authors.

At this point we should add a further word about the likely underrepresentation of professional and textbook writers in our sample. Curtis Benjamin, former chairman and president of McGraw-Hill Book Company, has argued that our sample largely excludes authors of what he calls "practical and professional books"—that is, a category consisting primarily of textbooks, professional treatises and reference works, and technical manuals. On this count he is undoubtedly correct, and his gross estimates of the large number of people who have a hand in writing such books, based on records of published titles, are at least reasonable, even if they seem to include an indeterminate number of salaried writers (not relying on royalties). However, his further assertion that the "success" of these authors invalidates the general conclusions of our study is highly dubious.[3]

This critic does not offer a single piece of evidence to counter our results. First, Benjamin does not indicate what the distribution of income is among the authors who he claims are underrepresented in our sample. He does provide gross figures on the total royalties paid by publishers of various types of trade books, professional books, and textbooks, but fails to give any reasonable estimate of how these royalties are distributed over the many authors who he sees making up this group.

The only figures for individuals cited in this analysis are based on Benjamin's probes of what "a few experienced textbook publishers know about payments to their own authors." Plainly, this is not a systematic technique of sampling: if his data are based upon "experienced textbook publishers," he is probably considering only the *crème de la crème*—the most successful publishing houses and the most successful authors. Had he made an adequate survey of the entire population of textbook authors at all publishing houses, as well as of those who had not had a text published in recent years, his estimates would undoubtedly be far lower.

Furthermore, even if we accept Benjamin's own rough estimate of the number of authors of practical and professional titles and textbooks, his analysis hardly suggests that we have underrepresented a disproportionately successful group. Figures reported by the Association of American Publishers for 1979 (representing approximately 85 percent of the industry's sales) suggest that about $131,900,000 in royalties were paid to authors of professional, school, and college textbooks. Again, using Benjamin's figures, if we divide the total number of authors who work in these genres into the total royalties paid, we find that, on average, an author of these types of books might expect to receive $381 for his or her work, which is far below the Authors Guild's reported median annual writing-related income of $4,715 for 1979. Even if we take Benjamin's remark that the total royalty figures he presents represent 60 percent of the total dollar sales of books in 1979 and inflate it to represent 100 percent of the sales, and then divide that figure by the total estimated number of authors working *only* in the professional books and textbook fields, we would obtain an average royalty figure for each author of $530 for 1979.

But, of course, these figures do not take into account, as they should, the distribution of incomes among authors of these types of books. Some textbook authors earn substantial sums, as is plainly indicated by Benjamin, but most probably do not. Yet if his data on the size of the author population and the distribution of royalties are at all instructive, they do not pose a convincing challenge to the validity of our survey. In sum, although there is underrepresentation of these authors in our sample, the effect is likely to lead to an *overestimation* of the writing-related income of authors.

It is also difficult to imagine that the exclusion of the pre-1976 invitees would upwardly bias overall figures relating to writing income. Many of the authors invited to join the guild before 1976 received a new invitation in the years 1976–79 with the publication of another book. (They were thus included in our sampling frame.) By and large, then, the authors who did not receive another invitation may be presumed to be relatively less prolific writers in recent years and, by extension, relatively less successful in financial terms. Again, this deficiency in our sampling frames may cause some *overstatement* in our estimates of the writing incomes received by authors.

Even with these limitations, the coverage of these sampling frames with respect to the population seems reasonably complete, especially among the types of authors who are of primary concern, that is, those seeking to appeal to a nonspecialist audience. With the noted exceptions of technical/academic writers and nonmembers without a publication in recent years, all groups of authors appear to be represented adequately.

SAMPLING STRATEGY AND SELECTION

To ensure an adequate total response for detailed statistical analysis, we decided on an overall sample size of about 5,000. This is an unusually large sample for a relatively small population. (In contrast, the size of the samples of the entire American population used by major survey organizations usually run between 1,500 and 2,500.) We selected such a large sample because we anticipated considerable difficulties in obtaining responses and because we wanted to guarantee a sufficient number of cases for reliable analyses of specific types of authors—in effect, subsamples of the sample.

Since we intended to ask for considerable information on that acutely sensitive subject, income, we also anticipated a certain reluctance in completing the questionnaire, especially among the nonmembers. Nonmembers owed no allegiance to the Authors Guild, and had little occasion to develop confidence in the guild's integrity. Even with firm guarantees of confidentiality, many of the nonmembers might therefore feel uncomfortable about divulging the requested information.

In deciding on sample strategy, we could not know what proportion of the total population of authors was represented by each sampling frame and thus sample so that all authors would have an equal chance of inclusion. Accordingly, our concern for securing a sufficient response directly affected the sampling procedures. Rather than merging the member and nonmember lists, we treated them as two separate sampling frames and sampled from them at slightly different rates. Nevertheless, each sample is still sufficiently large for us to judge whether the members of the guild differ significantly from the nonmembers in salient respects.[4]

Approximately 3,200 names were selected from the guild's membership list of some 5,000; the sampling ratio for the members was therefore about 60 percent. Somewhat fewer than 1,900 were selected from the list of invitees, a sampling ratio of about 50 percent. In both cases, we used a systematic sampling method whereby names were selected at regular intervals from the alphabetical lists.

Response

The success of the study hinged, of course, on obtaining the cooperation of the authors included in the sample. We had good reason to be concerned about the response rate, not merely because the questionnaire was fairly long but because it focused on income, a private matter for many people. We also feared that the "artistic temperament" of those in our sample might be resistant to the standardized format of a questionnaire.

Previous efforts to survey authors provided little cause for optimism. William J. Lord, Jr's 1962 study, *How Authors Make a Living: An Analysis of Free Lance Writers' Incomes 1953–1957*, is based on a survey of the Author League's members; the response rate was approximately 18 percent. In 1966, Richard Findlater published a pamphlet, *The Book Writers: Who Are They?*, which reported results of an investigation of the financial condition of members of Britain's Society of Authors. Fifty percent of the 3,240 members responded to the inquiry, of which 46 percent classified themselves as full-time authors and 10 percent as nearly full time. These data are reported in Hepburn (1968). More recently the staff of PEN, another organization of writers, sent a very short questionnaire to all the organization's members; 358 authors responded, a response rate of about 20 percent. Compared with the Author League's and PEN surveys, we were notably more successful in getting the cooperation of sampled authors. Subtracting the foreign and deceased members of the sample, as well as all with undeliverable addresses, our sample size was 4,856. Our analysis is based on 2,241 completed questionnaires, a response rate of 46 percent.[5]

This response represents the return from two mailings. Each respondent received an identification number which was attached to the questionnaire. Those identified as not responding to the first mailing were sent another questionnaire with a new letter asking for cooperation. We did not include any identifying marks on this second mailing because a considerable number of first wave respondents seemed to object to, or at least be wary of, the identification system.[6]

Of the completed questionnaires, 77 percent (n = 1730) were received on the first mailing, and the rest on the second. As expected, the guild members were the more cooperative; approximately 58 percent (n = 1833) of the members responded in contrast to 21 percent (n = 362) of the nonmembers.[7]

RESPONSE BIAS: SOME LIMITED CHECKS

Inferences about the population of authors as defined here rest, of course, on the "representativeness" of those responding to our survey. As we previously stated, there can be no direct test of the sample's representativeness because the population parameters are unknown. To reiterate, any claim to having obtained a representative sample must rest on two assumptions: that the sampling frames comprise a representative listing from the total population of freelance writers, and that the actual respondents constitute a random sample of the original sample. It is not possible to demonstrate conclusively that the first condition has been met, although major biases seem unlikely, as we have just noted. Consider now the second condition—whether the 46 percent of sampled authors who responded to the survey are themselves representative, that is, whether there is a response bias.

First, there is, in fact, no statistical basis for determining whether a certain response rate is acceptable: at issue is the representativeness of those who do respond, though a high rate usually reduces the chances of a serious response bias. (By usual standards of what is an acceptable response for a mail survey, our overall rate of 46 percent is low, but not unusually when sampling similar populations.) Furthermore, we initially put the word "representativeness" in quotes in this discussion to emphasize that a survey can be judged representative only in relation to specific characteristics of the respondents. In this survey, we are particularly interested in the accuracy of the data on income. A number of indirect indicators suggest that these data are accurate.

A recent, smaller-scale survey of authors provides one check on response bias. In the PEN survey of writers' income,[8] the median income from writing in 1979 was $4,700; the mean was $21,192. By comparison, the respondents of the Authors Guild survey had a median "total income directly related to writing" in 1979 of $4,775; the mean was $21,301. These figures are remarkably similar even though there are slight variations between the surveys in the formulation of the questions relating to income.[9] Such similarity adds some external validity to our findings.

We can also partially detect whether our sample included

a representative number of authors who achieved great success in the marketplace. This is a particularly important consideration because it is the financial bonanzas accruing to a few writers which seem to capture the public imagination. In reporting the "typical" story of writers' incomes, we want to be reasonably confident that our figures include the earnings of the financial superstars as well as the financially less successful. No single indicator of great success is beyond questioning, but authors whose books get on best-seller lists may be considered one indicator of the economic elite.

The percentage in the population of authors with best-sellers cannot be determined. To get a rough estimate, we tabulated the approximate percentage of new *titles* that made one of the *New York Times* best-seller lists (i.e., one of the top fifteen positions on the fiction or nonfiction hardcover lists or the mass or trade paperback lists) at any time in 1978 or 1979. In order to calculate the percentage, we counted the number of separate titles appearing on best-seller lists published in the *Times* and compared it with the number of new books published in each of these years taken from reports in *Publishers Weekly*. By this count, approximately 0.7 percent of the new books in each year made one of these lists. Of course, best-sellers need not get on a list in the same year in which they are published, but given the relative stability of the number of new books in these years and the similar percentage on best-seller lists; it seems likely that somewhat less than 1 percent of recently published books ever attain that enviable status.

Turning to our survey, we can report the percentage of authors (not titles) published in 1978 or 1979 who had a book on a *New York Times* best-seller list.[10] Obviously, this percentage is not directly comparable with that for titles. Some of the authors published in 1978–79 brought out more than one book in these years, and thus the percentage of recently published authors making a best-seller list should be somewhat higher than the percentage of new books achieving this status. Also, we have calculated the percentage of recently published authors with a best-seller over a two-year period (1978-79); but because the authors published in 1978 or 1979 certainly did not all publish a book in each year, half of this percentage is not necessarily an accurate one-year rate.

Nonetheless, since 4.5 percent of our respondents with a book published in 1978 or 1979 made a best-seller list in one of these years, we probably have not underrepresented the best-selling authors. We may crudely estimate that 3 percent of our respondents produced best-sellers, while about 1 percent of all books made one of these lists.

We also indirectly tested for response bias by comparing the distribution of responses in each mailing. In addition to sending a follow-up survey to those not responding to the first mailing, we subsequently sent a "miniquestionnaire" to a small, systematically drawn subsample of the nonresponding members of the guild. Even though the respondents to this third mailing had resisted two previous requests, we hoped that they would take the very short time necessary to check answers to a few questions. We selected questions from the main questionnaire that would allow us to judge whether these third-mailing respondents differed from respondents to each of the other mailings in certain critical respects.[11]

The logic of making this comparison rested on a supposition: if there were any distinctive factors causing nonresponse, the relatively reluctant respondents (as indicated by the mailing to which they responded) should be more like the nonrespondents (the completely reluctant) in these respects than the willing respondents. For instance, one might imagine that financially less successful writers were somehow embarrassed by their condition and were therefore disproportionately inclined not to complete the questionnaire. We could reasonably expect, however, that the later mailing might prompt a number of less successful writers to overcome their reluctance and complete the questionnaire. The proportion of writers with low incomes from writing would therefore increase with each mailing. Although we still could not know the actual proportion of such writers in the total population of authors, we might infer that completion of the questionnaire was related to degree of financial success and that the sample therefore underrepresented less successful writers. Correlatively, writers who earned a great deal from their books may have been reluctant to give us data on these earnings. Any increase in the proportion of financially successful writers in each mailing would suggest that the sample underrepresented the actual proportion of high earners. In short, it seemed plausible that our sample might underrepresent both extremes of the income distribution among authors. The third check of nonrespondents was aimed at testing these conjectures.

In any case, inferences based on the results of these procedures must necessarily be tentative, especially since we received, as might be expected, a very low response rate to the third mailing. Of a subsample of 154, responses numbered only 44, or 29 percent. Since this response was so small, we are still faced with a question of representativeness. That is, are these respondents to our third mailing representative of all other authors not responding to our first two mailings? We cannot be sure. The comparisons, while suggestive, cannot be the basis for a conclusive statement about response bias.

The details of this analysis are reported in appendix B. Suffice it to say that on nine separate items, ranging from productivity to 1979 writing-related income, the similarity of the respondents in the first and second mailings is unmistakable. If this analysis for response bias were based solely on a comparison of the large first two mailings, the likelihood of a significant bias would appear small. However, the addition of the very small number of third-mailing respondents introduces some doubts because they significantly differ from the second-mailing respondents in several respects (e.g., number of books published and recency of publication). Nevertheless, on perhaps the most crucial item, book-writing income, the difference between the second-and third-mailing respondents is not statistically significant, even at the .20 level. Thus our confidence in having obtained a representative sample of authors across the range of book-writing income is increased.

In sum, these limited checks for response bias all suggest that this survey neither underrepresents nor overrepresents financially successful authors. Three very different checks lead to this conclusion, enhancing confidence in the representativeness of the sample.

A COMPARISON WITH UNITED STATES CENSUS MATERIALS

While the definition of authors by the United States census which we previously presented makes it difficult to compare the incomes of authors in our sample with census figures, the census does provide data on the social composition of authors that furnishes some further tests of the adequacy of our sample. A strict comparison is not possible, but by relating some of the characteristics of our sample to data on authors in the 1970 and the 1980 censuses, we can obtain some clues about where our sample may be over-or underrepresenting the actual population of American authors.[12] Consider, then, several comparisons.

Of the 45,748 authors listed in the 1980 U.S. census (a 76 percent increase over the 1970 total), roughly 44 percent were women. In our sample, 40 percent were women. Furthermore, the educational achievements of authors in the 1970 census and our sample were similar: the median number of years of school completed by authors in the census was about 16, or approximately the equivalent of a college degree. For our sample, the median educational attainment was the receipt of a college degree. There were some differences between the geographical location of authors listed in the census and those in our sample. While roughly 21 percent of the authors in the 1970 census were located in New York City, 33 percent of the authors in our sample lived in the New York metropolitan area. However, when we add the numbers in smaller geographic areas close to the New York metropolitan area to the census figures for New York City, this differential is reduced by several percentage points.

The results of our survey and those obtained from the census are also similar in terms of the relationship between characteristics of authors and their earnings. For example, the relationship between gender and income and between geographic region and income were patterned in similar ways in our survey and in the census. The census data suggested somewhat larger overall median incomes for authors than we found in our survey, probably a consequence of the presence of editors and writers for broadcasting as well as authors of books in the census classification, and the inclusion in the census of all sources of income, rather than the more restrictive writing-related income that we used in our survey.

In fact, if we compare the median incomes of authors in the 1970 census who worked at least forty weeks during the year with our full-time authors (still not a strict comparison because the census does not specify whether this time was spent full time exclusively in writing-related activity), the figures are comparable. Our self-designated full-time authors earned roughly $10,900; those who worked at least forty hours a week had a median income from writing of $16,000 in 1979. The census figures for 1970 authors show a median income of $8,900 overall and $10,200 for those who worked at least forty weeks in 1969. Allowing for inflationary increases and some problems in consistent definitions of income and authorship, we still find figures that are similar. In short, the data from the census suggest that the sample of authors we generated through the Authors Guild is probably quite representative of the population of authors in the United States in terms of social characteristics, location, and general income parameters.

The Questionnaire

The report is primarily based on the results of a self-administered questionnaire, a reproduction of which appears in appendix A. Designing a survey of authors' incomes posed several problems. Questions relating to income and occupation in a survey of the general population, for example, are typically quite straightforward. Yet authors support themselves in many different ways and often have more than one occupation. Their various sources of income are also often related—e.g., freelance book-writing, fee-for-service editing, and salaried journalistic reporting—and therefore difficult to specify in clearly distinguishable categories. Indeed, the economic lives of some authors may be so complex that they can rightfully complain that standard questions relating to income and occupation do not fit their own circumstances.[13]

For the most part, the questionnaire consisted of precoded, closed-ended questions in which respondents were asked to check the most appropriate answer from a list of choices. Undoubtedly, structuring response categories meant that some particularities and nuances were overlooked or not given sufficient attention. But, as with censuslike questions generally, these closed-ended questions facilitated the statistical aggregation of responses. Such questions lent themselves to our analysis of certain characteristics of particular kinds of authors. We did ask respondents for brief comments on particular items and for remarks about their writing career. These written comments were helpful in analyzing and interpreting the statistical data. Finally, authors were not asked to provide exact income figures. That would have made the questionnaire too difficult to complete. Rather, they were asked to provide "your *best estimate* of the amount (pretax) that you received in each of the following categories."

The quality of the results depends, of course, on the accuracy of the self-reports made by the authors. No external checks can be made on the validity of the responses by the authors. If they are apt to distort their incomes, these distortions enter into our analysis. All surveys are subject to reporting error; one hopes that responses are not biased in a particular direction.

External checks on the validity of income-reporting in sample surveys are rare, but not unprecedented. One recent study provides some optimism about the accuracy of income-reporting. As part of the New Jersey Income-Maintenance Experiment, one of the most sophisticated social experiments ever conducted, Kershaw and Fair (1976) found a high correspondence between respondents' reports of income and government records of their income.[14] Plainly, it is not possible to know whether the authors in our survey were equally accurate (or, rather, consistent) in their reporting; but in the absence of any motivating impetus to bias results in a particular direction, this study does at least suggest that data on self-reported incomes should be taken seriously. We believe that, even on an ex post facto basis, it is difficult to convincingly interpret our income data as reflecting some consistent under- or overreporting.

To complement the analysis of the quantitative survey data, a dozen authors were interviewed at length either in person or on the telephone. The selected authors reflected differences in financial and critical success, age, sex, race, writing genre, work situation, and geographical location. These interviews ranged from a half hour to roughly two hours.

Largely unstructured and intended to probe the distinctive

Survey of American Authors

circumstances of each author's career, the interviews helped us interpret the quantitative analysis. But given the small number and the basis for selection, they were not particularly representative of authors in general or of particular types.

With these strengths and limitations of the survey in mind, we move to the central question of this study: what is the economic situation of American authors?

3.
The Writing Occupation

> Writing is a dog's life, but the only life worth living.
> Gustave Flaubert
>
> Writing is not a profession but a vocation of unhappiness.
> Georges Simenon
>
> They can't yank a novelist like they can a pitcher.
> A novelist has to go the full nine,
> even if it kills him.
> Ernest Hemmingway

CONSIDER THE CIRCUMSTANCES of these individuals, all of whom have published a book and therefore meet our definition of an author:

- A highly praised, award-winning novelist who writes virtually every day but has published only a handful of books, all with poor sales.
- A tenured university professor who concentrates on scholarly articles but has also written a few histories for more general audiences.
- A prolific, highly successful full-time writer of historical romances.
- A housewife with children who has written two mysteries in her spare time.

Any number of other examples could readily be produced to illustrate the great differences among the careers of authors. Plainly, it is difficult to portray these authors as belonging to a single occupation. An occupation may be sociologically defined as a relatively continuous and specific pattern of economic activity that provides workers with a livelihood and defines their social status.[1] Thus most accountants, like most firemen, do similar work, are accorded comparable social esteem, and are usually paid at roughly the same levels. In contrast, the differences in working conditions among writers seem as marked as their similarities.

For that reason our survey included several questions designed to distinguish among authors variously devoted to writing as an economic activity. By considering responses to these questions, we can systematically describe these variations. This is the main purpose of the present chapter. In the next chapter, "Income," we consider how the financial rewards of writing are related to varying commitments.

Levels of Work Commitment

The ranks of authors were about equally split between those who consider themselves full-time freelance authors or writers and those who do not. In response to the question "Would you characterize your occupation as full-time freelance author or writer?" just more than half replied affirmatively.

But self-designation as a full-time author may mean quite different things to different people. The authors were therefore asked to estimate the amount of time they devoted to writing: "On average, in the last year how many hours per week did you spend writing or directly working in some other way on your own book or article?" This question was deliberately worded so that authors would include research and thinking time, as well as time spent on other activities that directly contributed to their writing product.

The representative author, statistically indicated by the median, worked twenty hours a week at writing; that is, half of the authors worked more than twenty hours a week at writing, and half,

The Writing Occupation 43

TABLE 3.1. How Many Hours Authors Work Per Week:
A Comparison of Self-Designated Full-time and Part-time Authors

	Self-Designation	
Average hours per week writing	Full-time freelance author	Part-time freelance author
0–9	4%	33%
10–19	8	34
20–39	48	29
40+	40	5
TOTAL (rounded)	100%	101%
	(1038)	(1024)

less. The most active quarter of this sample of authors reported spending an average of thirty-five or more hours a week on writing; the least active quarter, fewer than ten.

Self-designated full-time and part-time authors differed substantially in the amount of time given over to writing (see table 3.1). Only 4 percent of the self-designated full-time authors worked fewer than ten hours per week, on average, compared with 33 percent of the self-designated part-time authors. Correlatively, fully 40 percent of these full-time, compared to 5 percent of these part-time, authors worked forty hours or more a week.

These different patterns were consistent with the widely noted fact that many authors supplement their writing incomes with money earned from other forms of work. In this sample of authors, almost half (46%) held "a paid position besides freelance writing" at the time of the survey, excluding occasional lectures or readings as well as irregular fee-for-service editing, translating, and so forth. (The distribution of positions is represented below in table 3.3) Thus, only a slight majority of authors can be occupationally defined solely by their writing activity.

Quite expectedly, the amount of time given to writing also differed substantially between those who held another job and those who only wrote (see table 3.2). More than three-quarters (77%) of the authors without another job wrote at least twenty hours a week; approximately a third wrote forty or more hours a week. In contrast, slightly more than half (57%) of those holding another job wrote fewer than twenty hours a week, while about half of this group wrote fewer than 10 hours a week. Nonetheless, many authors with another job still managed to give considerable, even large, commitments of time

TABLE 3.2. How Many Hours Authors Work Per Week:
A Comparison of Those with and Without Another Paid Position

	Occupational Commitment	
Average hours per week writing	Hold other paid job	No other paid job
0–9	28%	10%
10–19	29	13
20–39	34	43
40+	10	34
TOTAL (rounded)	101%	100%
	(983)	(1144)

to writing. The distinction between part and full-time authors is key, as will be demonstrated in chapter 4 where we examine their different economic rewards from writing.

However, in itself, the distinction between full time and part time can mask significant differences in the role of writing in the economic lives of authors. For example, both a semiretired seventy-year-old biographer and a homemaker with young children who writes juvenile fiction may be considered full time because they do not hold another paid position. Yet their time commitment to writing as an economic activity—whether by choice or necessity—is not as complete as, say, a prolific mystery writer who steadily writes six hours a day. By the same token, the young novelist who takes a one-course adjunct teaching job to subsidize a 30-hour writing work week may be considered a part-time author, even though her commitment to writing is more central to her life than that of the psychologist who has written two self-help books throughout his twenty-year professional career. There seems good reason, therefore, to take such variations into account as we examine the economic experience *within* the ranks of both full-time and part-time writers.

A Typology of Authors

These considerations suggest the value of a typology of authors based on their work patterns. The classification of authors that we developed

The Writing Occupation   45

is based on two aspects of authors' work lives: whether they held a regular, paid position other than writing, and the number of hours a week they spent in writing. Authors can be classified in any number of other ways; no one arrangement is uniquely right. Certainly commitment to writing might be gauged in ways other than the number of hours devoted to it. Many authors of talent and commitment have worked short hours. Still, we will see that a classification of aggregates of authors based in part on the average number of hours they devote to writing helps us analyze and understand the diversity of economic returns from writing.

The classification, or typology, is presented in figure 3.1:

FIGURE 3.1. A Typology of Authors

		Other Jobs	
		Do Not Hold Other Paid Position	Hold Paid Position Beside Freelance Writing
Average Number of Hours Devoted to Writing Per Week	25 or more hours	Committed Full-Timer Type I (35%)	Committed Part-Timer Type III (13%)
	10 to 24 hours	Limited Full-Timer Type II (19%)	Intermittent Part-Timer Type IV (21%)
	9 or fewer hours		Marginal Part-Timer Type V (13%)

Number of authors = 2,127.

Percent total 101 because of rounding errors.

Type I is the *committed full-time* author, who spends at least twenty-five hours a week on writing and holds no other paid position (though in some cases earning irregular fees-for-service—writing-related income from editing, translating, and the like). Thirty-five percent of all the authors are of this kind.

Type II, the *limited full-timer* (19 percent of the sample), consists of authors who report spending no more than twenty-five hours a week writing and hold no other regular paid job.

Type III, the *committed part-timer* (another 13 percent), holds a paid position other than freelance writing, and yet averages twenty-five or more hours a week on writing. This group of authors testifies to the commonplace that time is not a zero-sum phenomenon. In effect, these are authors who held two substantial positions.

Type IV, the *intermittent part-timer*, represents the sizable group of authors, 21 percent of them, who hold a paid position other than freelance writing, and devote a smaller but still considerable number of hours each week to their writing (ten to twenty-four hours).

Type V is the *marginal part-timer* (13 percent of all authors), who holds a paid position unconnected with the writing craft and puts in fewer than ten hours a week on writing.

Let us emphasize that this categorization only roughly indicates the extent to which authors are devoted to the occupation of book writing. It does not, of course, imply that the authors who give relatively little time to writing are any less serious about writing as an artistic, creative endeavor. Yet in terms of involvement in writing as work, there is clearly great diversity within the ranks of authors. Moreover, as we will see, these distinctions within the ranks of full- and part-time authors are often, though not invariably, associated with important differences in the economic lives of authors.

Full-timers: The On-and-Off Career

By asking authors to indicate their present occupational commitments, we in effect took a collective snapshot of the occupational distribution of authors at one point. As a result, this does not provide a sense of the highly irregular career patterns experienced by many authors. As one commented on the questionnaire, "I work (that is, hold another job) only when I have to." Just a few months earlier, then, he would have been considered a full-timer; at the time of the survey he was a part-timer.

Although all such career movements cannot be traced by data in hand, the limited information we do have on the occupational histories of the current full-timers is revealing. Most strikingly, less than a tenth of the full-timers were so throughout their working lives. Thus, this group of career-long, full-time writers represented about 5 percent of all authors. Moreover, most of the current full-timers relied on income from other jobs for considerable periods during their careers; in fact, half of them primarily supported themselves by other jobs for at least as many years as they have been full-time writers. On the other hand, almost half of the current part-timers were at one point or another full-timers for at least a year. And, indeed, several changes from part-timer to full-timer status were common.[2]

The occupational histories of the full-timers also make evident that writing is a career without any clearly specified entry-level position and associated career ladder. In most occupations there are reasonably clear pathways through the hierarchy of positions from beginning to high-ranking ones. In short, the reward system is patterned and reasonably well defined. An academic scientist has a well articulated road to move along from assistant to full professor. Lines of advancement are well articulated in other professions and in less prestigious occupations as well. However, writing as an occupation is different. The previous "other jobs" of the current full-timers were quite diverse, though the most common were teaching (16%), editor/publisher (19%), and "other professoinal" (27%). Relatively few worked at low prestige jobs; neither the shop floor nor the secretarial pool provided the start for many who turned to writing as a full-time job. The current committed and limited full-timers had virtually similar occupational backgrounds.

Let us be quite clear about our definition of full-time author. To reiterate: a significant number of those designated as full-timers took on other work—irregular, fee-for-service editing, translating, lecturing, etc. But this kind of work is often sporadic and frequently dovetails with their freelance writing. We therefore decided to distinguish such patterns of work from regular, salaried employment or professional/entrepreneurial endeavors in defining these types of authors. In fact, slightly more than 40 percent of both the committed and limited full-timers gave at least some time to these writing-related, fee-for-service activities. For some full-timers, these activities took up a good deal of time: 16 percent of the committed full-timers and 27 percent of the limited full-timers averaged at least ten hours a week.

In fact, 70 percent of all authors were engaged in some paid work other than book and article writing. Writing is an occupation, then, in which a sizable majority is actively engaged in some other paid work. Few authors work solely at writing throughout their careers to the total exclusion of other forms of regular employment. Indeed, since almost half of all authors held a regular other job, detailed consideration of the part-timers is essential to understanding this occupation.

Part-Time Authors: Their Occupations

For part-time writers, it often makes sense to talk of their *occupations* because their work lives are spread across two or more jobs. As one harried, New York-based novelist said in an interview, her work life has meant a time-pressed scramble across the metropolitan area—from one college to another to teach classes in writing, to a publishing company for editing work, and back home to take care of children and grandchildren. Many other writers have similar patterns of holding several jobs at once in order to support themselves. Although we cannot report all details of the occupational lives of this novelist and others like her, we can summarize the other kinds of paid jobs which provided part-time writers with the most income.

Table 3.3 indicates the kinds of other positions held by part-time authors. (Since variations by type of part-time author are slight, we simply consider all part-time writers together.) By far the most common ancillary occupation among part-time writers was university teaching. This is hardly surprising. Universities and colleges often provide a congenial environment for many kinds of writing. They allow for flexible hours, time off between semesters, library and other research facilities, and (sometimes) collegial encouragement. What is more, publication is frequently, in effect, a job requirement.

The second most common kind of work among part-time writers fell into that disparate category "other professional" which includes such varied occupations as lawyers, physicians, clergy, com-

The Writing Occupation

TABLE 3.3. Kinds of Other Paid Positions of Part-Time Authors

University teaching	36%
Editor/publisher	11
Journalist	5
Manager/proprietor	5
Primary/secondary school teaching	4
Clerical/secretarial	3
Blue collar/service	1
Sales/technical	3
Public relations	5
Other professional	20
Other	7
Total (rounded)	100%
	(1035)

puter programmers, and many kinds of "artistic" people. About a fifth of the part-time authors were in this occupational grouping. Although no great number appeared in any other single category, a substantial portion was employed in occupations which directly involved writing skills; "editor/publisher," "journalist," and "public relations" made up 21 percent of the total. By and large, then, most authors who held other jobs worked in relatively prestigious occupations, with a negligible few in blue-collar or lesser status white-collar occupations.

It is important to note here that writers, perhaps more than those in other "risky" professions such as dancers and artists, possess in their writing skills a portable and marketable commodity. Indeed, these skills may be marketable at a fairly good price. We shall see the extent to which this is so in our discussions of the economic returns to writers working at these other types of jobs.

NONWRITING WORK HOURS

The part-timers who gave relatively little time to writing—the intermittent and marginal group—worked considerable hours in their nonwriting jobs. Slightly more than half (55%) of the intermittent part-timers managed to work forty hours or more per week in some other job, as did two-thirds of the marginal part-timers. About 90 percent of each group worked at least twenty hours per week in their other jobs. By contrast, the committed part-timers generally had other jobs that imposed relatively modest time demands; a quarter of the committed part-timers held jobs that took up fewer than ten hours a week.

In terms of the relative allocation of time, the marginal part-timers typically devoted eight times as many hours a week to their other jobs as to their writing; the intermittent part-timers, about two-and-a-third times. In decided contrast, the committed part-timers were generally authors first: for every hour spent in some other job, they spent two on writing.[3]

Attitudes toward the Mixed Career

Part-time authors have mixed careers of diverse sorts, usually, it seems, as a matter of economic necessity more than of preference. A sizable proportion of authors suggested that they did not find their jobs especially satisfying. For example, to the question "If you could at least match your present total income by writing full-time, would you drop your other work?" almost half (46%) of the part-time authors responded "yes" and another 22 percent "possibly." Given the opportunity to support themselves fully from writing, most of these authors would have reapportioned their work time to give greater emphasis to writing.

However, the part-timers' feelings about their other jobs were related to its type. More than 60 percent of the part-time authors who worked as clerical workers, primary and secondary school teachers, sales/technical workers, or managers/proprietors expressed the desire to give up their other jobs and write full time if they could match their present income. University teachers exhibited the greatest hesitancy to make such a change in work pattern. Only a third indicated that, considerations of income aside, they would prefer to become full-time writers.

This generally strong preference for writing among the part-timers was suggested by another result from the survey (see table 3.4.) When we asked "How do you evaluate the personal satisfaction

The Writing Occupation

TABLE 3.4. How Part-time Authors Rate the Satisfaction of Writing vs. Their Other Jobs

	Type of Part-Time Author			
Relative job satisfaction[a]	Committed part-timers	Intermittent part-timers	Marginal part-timers	Total
Other job much more satisfying	1%	4%	6%	4%
Other job somewhat more satisfying	0	1	5	2
About equally satisfying	23	29	41	31
Writing somewhat more satisfying	9	8	8	8
Writing much more satisfying	65	55	36	53
Not sure	2	2	3	2
Total (rounded)	100%	99%	99%	100%
	(247)	(422)	(261)	(730)

[a]Responses to "How do you evaluate the personal satisfaction of writing as compared to your other work?"

of writing as compared to your other work?" approximately three-quarters of the committed part-timers and almost two-thirds of the intermittent part-timers reported that they found writing "much more satisfying" or "somewhat more satisfying" than their other jobs. These writers rarely expressed any preference for their other work. Only the aggregate of marginal part-timers wavered in their preference: fully 41 percent found their other work as satisfying as writing, and another 11 percent actually found the other work "more" satisfying.

It comes as no surprise, then, that the chief reason for taking on paying work besides writing was financial. In response to the question "What is your *primary* motivation for having paying work besides book or article writing?" approximately two-thirds of the committed and intermittent part-timers indicated that they held another job because it provided "necessary income for living" or "a desirable complementary source of income."[4] Even among the marginal part-timers, only a third responded in a way that suggested any positive attachment to their other work that went beyond considerations of income.

Although most part-time authors were not particularly happy with their other jobs, almost three-quarters of them considered them "relatively permanent." Only a tenth definitely thought that their present other jobs—or at least ones like them—lacked permanence.

Whatever their hopes or preferences to the contrary, then, the great majority of part-timers expected to continue in mixed occupational careers.

How does holding another job affect an author's writing? The most obvious effect is on time. Even if time is considered in variable rather than fixed terms, and even if we admit to different levels of energy and efficiency among writers, at a point the more time spent on an ancillary job means less time available for writing. Other jobs reduced the blocks of time that could be devoted to their work as writers. As indicated in interviews and written comments on the questionnaire, many authors holding other jobs agreed with the comment made by one young author-professor who said "Of course I would be more productive if I had more time." And as a well-respected writer emphasized in an interview, time off the ancillary job is not necessarily time available for writing. While working in advertising for a number of years, he held jobs that were not "too taxing" but still required considerable concentration and effort. His job "could not be 'left' at the work place"; it "carried over," requiring an effort for the writer to unwind emotionally. Only through "self-conscious discipline" could he begin to write effectively "in my own voice."

The limited number of authors we interviewed were not all of one mind on the question of how ancillary jobs affected the quality of their writing. Two well-known novelists expressed completely opposite views. One maintained that "writers should have a job; writing isn't a job." She believed that work on her other job helped to keep her mentally sharp and in touch with how others think. But as she was quick to add, her situation was unusual since she held a responsible job which afforded a good deal of time for writing. For her, writing was a distinct luxury— "I would write for myself even if I wasn't published"—a luxury which should not be overindulged. Just as emphatically, the second novelist believed "other work is death to writing; a writer needs to be obsessive." From time to time, however, she felt compelled by financial pressures to teach writing on a part-time basis. She kept these responsibilities to a minimum in the belief that she would be "a better and more productive writer" as a result. To judge from notes in the margins of many questionnaires, the attitude expressed by the second author quoted here was quite common among

The Writing Occupation

part-time writers, certainly more so than the view of the first novelist. But these remain as assertions and speculations from a relatively small number of authors, and the contending beliefs about the consequences for writing of other work remain to be examined in detail.

Whatever the effect on writing quality, many part-time authors wrote comments that seemed to express a fatalistic acceptance of their mixed careers. Part-time authors did not suggest they held other jobs in search of "material." One young, well-educated novelist who had some blue-collar jobs indicated that their chief appeal was not "the experience which they provide." Although he has written movingly about blue-collar workers, he said only: "The jobs were available, I needed some money, and I could go home at night and write and concentrate on it."

In sum, the men and women who write books are plainly a diverse group. Their patterns and habits of work, as well as their commitment to writing, differ markedly. Furthermore, the kinds of supplementary work which they take on also vary greatly. Therefore, to speak of authors as a single group can only be misleading. A study of the income of authors requires, then, that we consider the writing-related income and auxilliary income associated with several types of authors. An instructive analysis of the economic conditions of book authors must take into account these differing commitments to writing and to other jobs.

4.

Income

> The profession of book-writing makes horse racing seem like a solid, stable business.
> John Steinbeck

> You must never suppose, because I am a man of letters, that I never tried to earn an honest living.
> George Bernard Shaw

CONSIDERING THE DIVERSITY of authors' occupational lives, there is no single, clear-cut way to state how authors fare financially. To assess their economic return from writing may be largely a matter of adding up checks for royalties and any subsidiary rights. But to evaluate their overall financial condition, the results in chapter 3 indicate that we must take into account the various sources of authors' income.

In examining the economic conditions of authors, we therefore focus on two distinct questions. The first and principal one is, What is the writing-related income of different types of authors? The second is, What is the total income of authors, including income from writing, other jobs, and from other family members? Plainly, as our summary in chapter 1 indicated, most authors would find themselves in a state of virtual poverty if they had to depend solely on their writing income, but most also do far better economically largely because of their ability to earn money in other ways. The point is not to focus only on one or the other of these economic indicators. Separately they answer different questions; together they give us a larger picture of the financial status of American authors. Thus, the discussion of authors' incomes will have two major sections.

In the first section we examine the economic return from writing, with special attention to variations among the five types of authors described in chapter 3. We also consider contributions of various sources of writing income to total writing income, fluctuations in writing income, and the social and writing career correlates of such income. In the second section we report data on total personal and family income, including the relative contributions of writing and nonwriting income. Writers' incomes are also compared with other occupational groups.

A critical cautionary note is in order. Although we will report a number of summary measures—e.g., median total family income in 1979—these figures represent an incomplete story. The great number of nonaverage writers are equally deserving of notice. The variance in authors' incomes is large. Therefore, the representation and portrayal of their economic condition through the use of statistical averages must fail by definition to capture the high level of variability in the economic lives of authors.[1]

Writing Income

Even a cursory examination of the income schedule (questionnaire, appendix A, pp. 172–173) suggests that many authors would not find it simple to record their writing-related income. Since the term "writing-related" could have meant different things to different authors, we defined it—necessarily at length—as the total earned in a calendar year from royalties from hardcover editions, paperback originals, and paperback reprints; all other subsidiary rights; fees for freelance magazine and newspaper articles; and payments for television, radio, and movie scripts. We explicitly excluded all earnings from salaried jobs,

Income

even if the work involved writing (e.g., newspaper reporter), as well as freelance fee-for-service editing, translating, lecturing, etc. (We have separate estimates of these sources of income.) Plainly, active authors who write for several media and have a "hot" book must keep track of a complicated and irregular flow of money. Even if the amounts are not large, a considerable number of checks for various royalty payments and subsidiary rights, in addition to the occasional article, must be tabulated. The total income from all these writing-related sources provided us with our best estimate of the author's income from writing.

In 1979, the representative (i.e., median) author in this survey earned a total of $4,775 from writing.[2] In short, half of American authors actually earned less than $5,000 from their writing in that year. A quarter of all writers earned $1,000 or less, and a tenth reported no income at all from writing in that year. The top 10 percent of writing income exceeded $45,000 in 1979; the writing income of the top 5 percent exceeded $80,000. But these were the rarified few. The central message of this study appeared almost at the outset: most authors can not begin to make ends meet from their writing alone.

This general picture can be seen from another perspective. Figure 4.1 sets out the proportions of authors in the sample located in seven income groups, ranging from the 10 percent who in 1979 earned nothing at all and the additional 28 percent receiving up to $2,500 that year to the 4 percent with incomes of $100,000 or more. Again, the pattern is clear: the many in the lowest groups receiving negligible income from their writing and the few at the top being very highly rewarded.

Relating the number of hours that authors worked at writing to their incomes from that work, we can arrive at a rough estimate of median hourly income rate in 1979—just under five dollars an hour ($4.90).[3] Only a quarter of the authors earned as much as $15.00 an hour, and an equal number worked for about a dollar or less. Only a small minority, 10 percent, made an "hourly wage" of at least $40.00 per hour. If this figure represented the top of the profession, it is one that still pales in comparison to the $200 or more that top lawyers at major law firms billed per hour.

To put these writing wages in perspective, the authors' 1979 median hourly income from writing of $4.90 was lower than the

**Figure 4.1: 1979 Writing-Related Income
Percentage Distribution of Authors by Income Category**

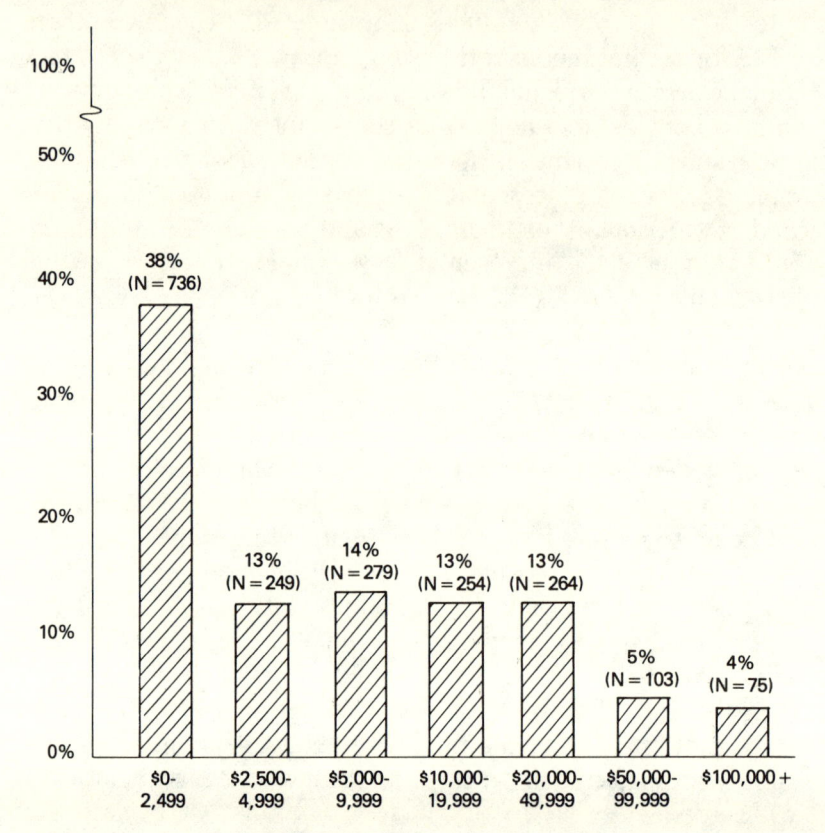

Income Category	Percentage	N
$0-2,499	38%	736
$2,500-4,999	13%	249
$5,000-9,999	14%	279
$10,000-19,999	13%	254
$20,000-49,999	13%	264
$50,000-99,999	5%	103
$100,000+	4%	75

$6.54 rate paid to production and related workers in manufacturing. The median hourly pay for such workers in mining, contract construction, and transportation was even higher. Specific comparisons with various types of unionized craftsmen are also telling. The median of some $4.90 an hour for writers compared with $11.72 for painters, $10.95 for bricklayers, $10.48 for building laborers, $8.85 for tile layer's helpers, and $8.25 for elevator constructor's helpers.[4]

Plainly, then, writers must subsidize themselves with other forms of work; indirectly they may also be subsidizing the publishing industry. Recently, James Lincoln Collier made just this claim. Using himself as an example, Collier described his income and expenses

Income   59

from the publication of his widely acclaimed book, "The Making of Jazz," which was an American Book Award nominee, which the *New Yorker* called "an essential book," and which *Publishers Weekly* called "now the finest book of its kind."

My income to date from the book is $27,884. There was no agent's fee, but deducting 25% for overhead and fringe, mainly retirement fund, I have $20,913 left. I also spent $1,500 for photographs, $1,000 for travel for research and promotion, $400 for 100 books, $1,500 for 300 records, leaving $16,413. I spent two years writing the book, over a span of four years. Thus, my annual before-tax income from it was $8,200. And even if you forget about overhead and fringe, I still made only $14,000 a year from the book, before taxes. In terms of time that might have been spent in more profitable ways, the book cost me several tens of thousands of dollars out of my own pocket to write. (1981:22)

Collier goes on to conclude, using the result of this survey:

This is the crux of the matter: according to the Guild survey, median hourly income for writers is $4.90. Nobody else in the publishing business works for those wages. Writers know that publishing profits are down, and that editors are poorly paid. But publishers do make money, editors eat and pay their rent, printers expect to retire on a pension. Most writers have no hope of any of these things. (1981:23)

SOURCES OF WRITING INCOME

For all the public notice given to the diverse and sometimes spectacularly lucrative money-making avenues open to authors, most authors still make virtually all their writing-related income from books, especially from royalty payments. The typical author received 98 cents of every writing dollar from books, including both royalty payments and all subsidiary rights.[5] Royalty payments alone typically accounted for 87 cents of every writing-related dollar. For a quarter of the authors, however, royalty payments constituted less than half of their writing income, and, correspondingly, other sources of such income were relatively important for them.[6]

Subsidiary Rights. A few authors make huge sums on the sales of their books to films or magazines, but their good fortune is hardly typical. Indeed, a few respondents to our survey reported such huge sums from subsidiary rights, but the representative author derived no money whatsoever from all subsidiary rights to books. The median income from those rights was zero. (This figure holds for each of the five types of authors.) Only about a tenth of all authors made as much as $2,000 in 1979 from subsidiary rights. Of course, many recognized the possible rewards of having a movie option picked up—"That's my big hope, my real chance to get security," one mystery writer believed—but very few achieved them. Only a tenth of all authors made as much as 20 percent of their writing income from subsidiary rights.

Articles and Scripts. The book author who successfully turns to articles or script writing is most uncommon. The median income from article writing for all full-timers and both intermittent and marginal part-timers was zero; the figure among committed part-timers was $228. The median income from script writing (including films, television, and radio) for all five types of authors was also zero.

While most authors garnered nothing from magazine or newspaper articles, these outlets were of paramount importance to some. A tenth of all authors—with only slight variation among the five types—earned virtually all their writing income from freelance magazine and newspaper articles. For a quarter, moreover, article writing provided about a third of their total writing income. For a notable minority, then, article writing did not so much define their writing activities as represent a significant, complementary form of work.

Few authors derived a substantial percentage of their incomes from script writing. Approximately 1 percent earned their writing income primarily from fees for scripts, and roughly one in twenty earned more than a third of his or her writing income from script writing.

INCOME FLUCTUATIONS

The writing incomes of many authors fluctuate notably, even on a year-to-year basis. As one author wrote to us, "No year is typical in a writer's career; the ups and downs and precariousness are well known." Another echoed these sentiments: "There are good years

Income

and bad years and there could be years of no income at all." Table 4.1 indicates this flucuation. The 1978 writing incomes of authors (expressed in 1979 purchasing power) are cross-tabulated with 1979 writing incomes.

The great majority (82%) of writers with low incomes ($0-2,499) in 1978 remained in the same income category in 1979, and writers who enjoyed substantial financial success in 1978 (100,000+) were apt to repeat this success (87%) in 1979. Between these extremes, however, the 1979 writing incomes of authors often varied substantially from their 1978 level. Upward and downward movement was common. However, inspection of the data in table 4.1 indicates that an author who earned anywhere in the wide range from $5,000 to $99,999 in 1978 was slightly more likely to move to a lower than a higher income level in 1979. For instance, of authors who earned somewhere between $5,000 and $10,000 in 1978, 23 percent experienced an increase, 48 percent stayed at the same level, and 29 percent had a drop in writing income.

The frequent fluctuations in writing incomes are also apparent in a comparison of authors' 1979 writing incomes with those in their "best year" (adjusted to 1979 dollars). Table 4.2 makes clear that only a minority of authors were able to match even roughly their best year income in 1979, and many earned far less. Consider the 1979 income of the authors who at some prior point in their career received $20,000–49,999 from writing—a level certainly encompassing a large range but hardly spectacular success. Less than two out of five reached this level of success in 1979, and a quarter dropped below $5,000.

Seen another way, half of all authors earned at least 1.7 times more from writing in their best year than in 1979. (That is, the median of the ratios of best year writing income to 1979 writing income is 1.7.) Compared with 1979 writing income, a fourth of all writers earned 4.5 times as much in their best year, and a tenth earned fully 15 times as much. All these relative changes in writing income should not obscure the fact that the amounts earned in the best years were typically modest. Generally, it was not a matter of "feast or famine," as one author described his situation, because chronic famine was the more common condition.

And yet, most authors did not have to look too far in the past for their best year. For all age groups up to sixty-five, authors tended

TABLE 4.1. Year-to-Year Fluctuations: How Much Authors Made from Writing in 1978 and 1979

1978 Writing Income[a]

1979 Writing Income	$0–2,499	$2,500–4,999	$5,000–9,999	$10,000–19,999	$20,000–49,999	$50,000–99,999	$100,000+	Total
$0–2,499	82%	32%	12%	8%	2%	1%	—	38%
$2,500–4,999	9	42	17	4	1	—	2	13
$5,000–9,999	5	15	48	17	4	3	—	14
$10,000–19,999	3	8	15	47	15	—	—	13
$20,000–49,999	1	1	7	21	61	25	5	14
$50,000–99,999	—	1	1	3	14	56	7	5
$100,000+	—	—	—	—	3	14	87	4
Total (rounded)	100%	99%	100%	100%	100%	99%	101%	101%
	(709)	(267)	(286)	(277)	(234)	(91)	(61)	(1925)

[a] 1978 income is adjusted to 1979 dollars.

TABLE 4.2. How Much Authors Made From Writing in Their Best Year vs. 1979

Income in Best Year (adjusted for inflation)

1979 Writing Income	$0–2,499	$2,500–4,999	$5,000–9,999	$10,000–19,999	$20,000–49,999	$50,000–99,999	$100,000+	Total
$0–2,499	100%	69%	47%	32%	16%	10%	12%	37%
$2,500–4,999	—	31	20	17	9	3	3	13
$5,000–9,999	—	—	33	19	17	10	4	15
$10,000–19,999	—	—	—	32	19	13	6	13
$20,000–49,999	—	—	—	—	39	30	19	14
$50,000–99,999	—	—	—	—	—	34	14	5
$100,000+	—	—	—	—	—	—	43	4
Total (rounded)	100%	100%	100%	100%	100%	100%	101%	101%
	(150)	(202)	(280)	(336)	(390)	(173)	(133)	(1664)

to have their best year within the last few years; less than a tenth enjoyed their best year more than a decade ago. The writers aged sixty-five or more, however, typically had their best year in 1970, and a quarter had their best year almost a decade before then.

All this fluctuation, one can well imagine, creates practical difficulties for authors in managing their financial affairs, to say nothing of related anxieties. One author reported his efforts to take it in stride: "My income was $51,000 in 1978 and $7,000 in 1979. I decided to take 1978 as the typical year and treat 1979 as a most untypical one." Whether many can muster such equanimity and even optimism in light of such circumstances is surely doubtful.

Occupational Commitment and Income

The overall figures on writing income certainly point to a depressing state of affairs for authors—and certainly little encouragement to the prospective author. Yet as we emphasized in the previous chapter, those meeting our inclusive definition of an author are a highly disparate group. We now sharpen the focus on writing income to consider this diversity.

Indeed, it could be argued that many authors cannot reasonably hope for much financial reward from their writing if only because they cannot—or at least, do not—devote much time to it. As previously noted, almost half (46%) of the authors sampled were holding paid positions in addition to working on their freelance writing. Understandably enough, this competing commitment cut into writing time and income. The median income from writing among those with another job was some $2,700; for authors without other paid jobs, it was about three times as large, $8,000.

The contrasts in income were even more striking between the writers who saw themselves as full-time authors and the rest. The median income in 1979 of these self-designated full-time authors was

Income

Figure 4.2. Time Commitment and 1979 Writing Income

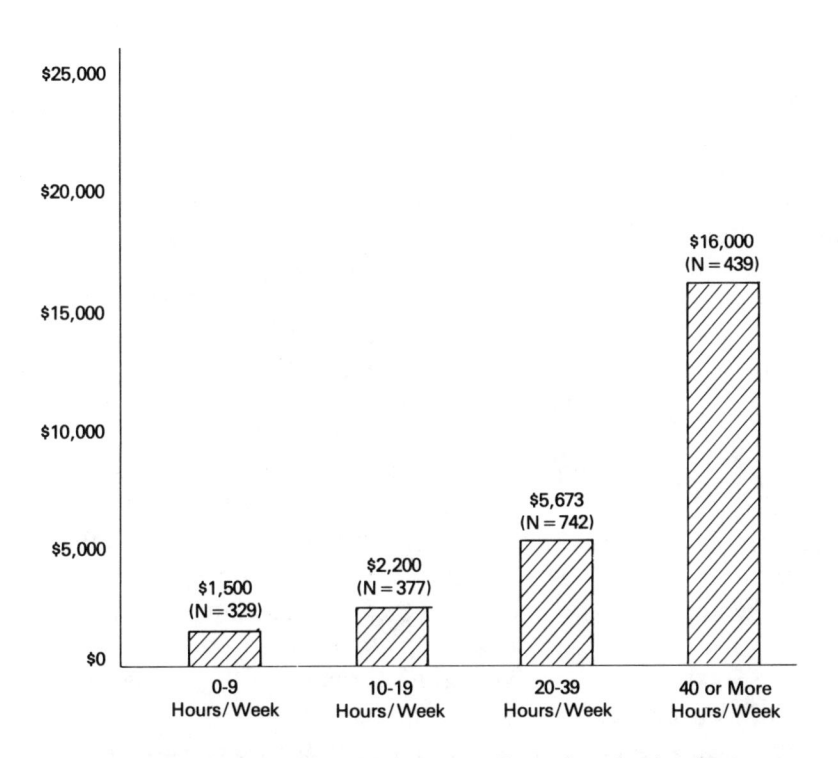

[Bar chart showing median 1979 writing-related income by hours/week:
- 0-9 Hours/Week: $1,500 (N=329)
- 10-19 Hours/Week: $2,200 (N=377)
- 20-39 Hours/Week: $5,673 (N=742)
- 40 or More Hours/Week: $16,000 (N=439)]

The dollar figures are the median 1979 writing-related income for authors in each category of average number of hours spent writing per week.

more than five times larger than that of the self-designated part-time authors: roughly $10,900 compared to $2,000.

As we might suppose, the authors who spent very few hours on their writing had very low writing incomes, as is evident in figure 4.2. We might also suppose that those who devoted a good deal of time to their writing might have reaped the financial benefits. Not so. Even among the 23 percent of authors who worked at least forty hours a week at their writing, half earned less than $16,000 in 1979. For the rest, putting in variously less time on their craft, the income from writing fell off dramatically.

THE FIVE TYPES AND WRITING INCOME

These variations in writing income may be further detailed in terms of our typology of authors (portrayed in figure 3.1 on page 45). Table 4.3 presents the distribution of 1979 writing income for each author type. The intermittent and marginal part-timers plainly earned very little from writing, with half of the former and almost two-thirds of the latter receiving less than $2,500. The committed full-timers were much more likely than all other types to exceed this amount; almost 80 percent did so. In turn, the committed part-timers (68%) were more likely than the limited full-timers (59%) to exceed this paltry sum. Turning to the other extreme of the income distribution, we see that 38 percent of the committed full-timers earned at least $20,000 in 1979 from writing, compared with 25 percent of the committed part-timers, 18 percent of the limited full-timers, and much lower rates among the other types.

Figure 4.3 presents the median income from writing in 1979 for the five types of authors. The committed full-time authors earned the highest incomes from writing, approximately $11,000. But the limited full-timers who devoted fewer than twenty-five hours a week to writing typically made only $3,370. These limited full-timers earned substantially less on average than those committed part-timers ($6,000) who put in more than twenty-five hours a week. The marginal part-time authors who average fewer than ten hours at writing a week typically earned almost nothing from their publications.

These distributions suggest that the amount of time devoted to writing is a somewhat stronger determinant of writing-related income than is the existence of another paying job. And, indeed, as the zero-order correlation coefficients reported in table 4.4 indicate, the average number of hours a week spent writing was more strongly associated with 1979 writing income (and three transformations of this figure) than full-time status.[7] The respective correlations with income (untransformed) are .21 and .13. Furthermore, a multiple regression analysis, including these and other factors related to income, suggests that time spent at work on writing is the more important of the two correlates of writing income. Indeed, other than recency of publication, of all the variables considered in the analysis, the sheer

TABLE 4.3. How Much The Five Types of Authors Earned from Writing in 1979

1979 Writing-Related Income

Author Type	$0–2,499	$2,500–4,999	$5,000–9,999	$10,000–19,999	$20,000–49,999	$50,000–99,999	$100,000+	Row total
Committed full-timers	21	8	16	16	23	8	7	99% (661)
Limited full-timers	41	18	10	13	9	6	3	100% (330)
Committed part-timers	32	13	17	13	16	6	3	100% (238)
Intermittent part-timers	49	15	17	11	5	1	1	99% (403)
Marginal part-timers	64	14	9	8	3	1	—	99% (239)

Note: Percentages represent the proportion within each author type with an income corresponding to each income category. Percentages for each type add across to 100% (allowing for discrepancies caused by rounding).

Figure 4.3: How Much Our Five Types of Authors Earned from Writing in 1979

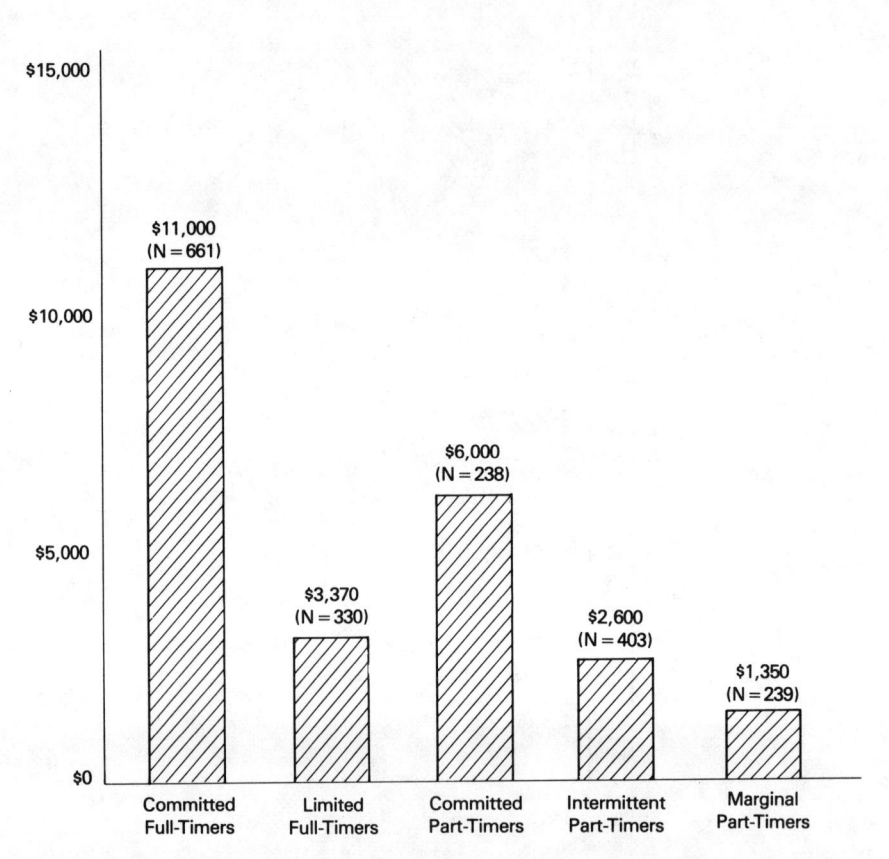

Author Type	Median Income	N
Committed Full-Timers	$11,000	661
Limited Full-Timers	$3,370	330
Committed Part-Timers	$6,000	238
Intermittent Part-Timers	$2,600	403
Marginal Part-Timers	$1,350	239

The dollar figures are the median 1979 writing-related income.

number of hours devoted to the trade had the strongest net effect on writing income.[8]

While hours spent writing is modestly associated with writing income, this finding should not be misinterpreted. Long hours of writing are surely no guarantee of high income. Recall that even among the 23 percent of authors who worked at least forty hours a week at their writing, the median 1979 writing income was $16,000.

Income

TABLE 4.4. Zero-Order Correlations Between Writing Income (Raw Values and Three Transformations) and Selected Variables

	1979 writing income	Log of 1979 writing income[1]	Collapsed income[2]	Log of collapsed income[3]	N
Paternal occupation[a]	−.05	−.04	−.04	−.04	1,771
Paternal education[b]	−.02	.03	.00	.03	1,903
Have relative author[c]	−.05*	−.05*	−.05*	−.05*	1,914
Education[d]	−.07*	−.06*	−.11*	−.05*	1,914
Prestige of education[e]	−.05	−.01	−.03	−.01	1,674
Race[f]	.01	.03	.01	.03	1,911
Gender[g]	.04	.04	.09*	.04	1,926
Hours/week writing	.21*	.32*	.36*	.31*	1,883
Hours/week other job	−.16*	−.23*	−.27*	−.22*	1,829
Full-time status[h]	.13*	.18*	.25*	.17*	1,942
Recency of publication[i]	−.13*	−.39*	−.21*	−.39*	1,646
Number of books	.13*	.24*	.26*	.24*	1,930
Honor[j]	.05*	.15*	.11*	.15*	1,757
Writing experience[k]	.00	−.01	.01	−.01	1,520
Age	−.01	−.14*	−.07*	−.14*	1,747
Genre fiction[l]	.13*	.07*	.16*	.06*	1,895
Adult fiction[l]	.06*	−.05*	.09*	−.06*	1,895
Adult nonfiction[l]	−.03	.03	−.02	.03	1,960
Children's books[l]	−.03	.04	−.04	.04*	1,960
All other genres[l]	−.10*	−.06*	−.13*	−.06*	1,895

*All starred correlations are significant at .05 level.

Notes: (1) Authors reporting zero income were coded #1. (2) All authors with incomes above $80,000 (the top 5% in the sample were coded as $80,000). (3) Log of the values in the second transformation.
a) 1 = blue-collar/service; 2 = lower white-colar; 3 = manager/professional.
b) Five values: less than high school through postcollege degree.
c) 1 = yes; 0 = no.
d) Seven values: less than high school through Ph.D.
e) 1 = no college; 2 = nonprestigious college; 3 = prestigious college.
f) 1 = white; 0 = all other races.
g) 1 = male; 0 = female.
h) 1 = hold no other job; 0 = hold other job.
i) 1 = 1977–1980; 2 = 1970–76; 3 = pre-1970.
j) 1 = no award; 2 = minor award winner; 3 = major award winner.
k) (1980−[year of first book publication]). E.g., 1980−1962 = 18.
l) Dummy variables for genre; 1 = specified genre; 0 = all other genres.

Moreover, the causal nature of this relationship is far from clear. On the one hand, extra time may increase the amount of writing produced and hence prospects for financial reward. But just as conceivably, certain authors may be able to "afford" to give relatively long hours to writing because they have been financially well rewarded in the past. That is, hours writing and writing income may be the mutual concomitants of success.

In short, neither long hours devoted to writing nor a single-minded occupational commitment to it—nor indeed both together—provide any guarantee of modest recompense. And yet it is only those authors who make an intense occupational commitment to writing who typically have even a reasonable chance of supporting themselves as writers. All others generally face bleak prospects. The general economic problem of authors results not from a lack of effort devoted to their work but from a lack of pay for that effort.

Personal Characteristics, Writing Careers, and Earnings

We now turn to how social backgrounds and personal characteristics, as well as certain aspects of authors' writing careers, are related to writing income. In effect, we ask here, How is economic success within this occupation socially patterned? Does information about an author's social background, personal characteristics, or writing career provide any clue as to how she or he is economically rewarded as a writer?

Social scientists have repeatedly shown that personal attributes such as family background (that is, parental education and economic standing), native aptitude, personal educational achievement, race, and sex are related to chances of economic success in the general population (see, for example, Jencks et al. 1979). For some of these variables, such as educational achievement, the influence is strong and direct. For others, such as family background, the influence comes principally from the effect that such a background has on a person's own educational achievement. Other job-related influences, such as tenure, seniority, or years of experience also help to predict earnings.

Most of this research has focused on the incomes of individuals variously located throughout the entire occupational structure of the United States. Far less work has been carried out on the prediction of income differences among individuals working in the same occupation. Here we ask, Do these factors that are effective in predicting income differences in society-at-large also help us to better understand variations in authors' incomes? Our analysis, then, complements an emerging research concern for explaining *intra*occupational success.

Given the great number of authors with very low or no income whatsoever from writing, however, it should be evident that any attempt to explain variation in income systematically can provide us with only limited results. The overriding fact is that, whatever the authors' personal characteristics, the dollar differences separating the large majority are quite small, if not trivial. The subsequent analysis should be considered within this context.

We take up in turn a number of factors which we consider as part of an author's "characteristics" and then others which we classify as part of the author's "career history." Of course, these statistical relationships are limited in their value in yet another sense. They cannot fully capture the complex influences of race, sex, religion, and other social characteristics on the experiences of writers. At best, they provide us with a skeleton without flesh, but one which does have the broad outlines of the correlates of differential income among authors.

The data in table 4.4 provide a quick statistical summary of how a number of personal characteristics and social statuses are related to writing income. However, in the subsequent discussion, we also consider in some detail the relative probabilities of reaching certain income levels for authors with different characteristics. This discussion is intended to be understandable to readers without statistical training.

PERSONAL CHARACTERISTICS

Family Background. To state the matter briefly, the effect of family background attributes—paternal occupation and education—

on the financial success of writers is almost nil. Consider several examples. Authors whose fathers were blue-collar workers or farmers are as apt to enjoy substantial financial success ($50,000 or more) in writing as are the authors whose fathers worked in white-collar jobs. Correlatively, the likelihood of financial success through writing is about equally small for all authors, whatever their family background.

Indeed, even authors with a relative in the profession are no more likely than others to be financially successful. Of course, an individual's writing career might be furthered substantially because of a relative's prominence in writing circles, but simply being from a writing family does not provide any financial edge. The absence of such a family advantage among writers stands in distinct contrast to well-established "inheritance effects" and benefits among the children of business executives in America and to some extent also among politicians, members of the military, and even scientists. In fact, if authors are the sons and daughters of authors, this legacy might be characterized as an inheritance of poverty.

Parental education has a similarly low association with financial rewards in writing. Whatever cultural advantages the relatively educated may pass on to their children, they do not translate into distinctively good chances for financial success in writing. The educational attainment of authors' parents confers neither a head start nor a liability.

Education of Authors. A similar conclusion holds for the education of authors themselves. The correlation between education and financial reward for writing is virtually zero. College graduates fare no better no average than those with less formal education. Although it may appear that a negative association actually exists between education and income here (Ph.D's are somewhat less likely than those authors with less formal education to earn more than $5,000 from their writing), this is probably an artifact of the lesser commitment among holders of the Ph.D., who are usually professors, to the publication of trade books.

Among the college educated, the prestige of an author's alma mater is unrelated to the economic returns of writing.[9] This finding runs counter to the general pattern in American society, in which degrees from the most prestigious colleges appear to have greater financial payoff—either because the more talented youngsters choose and are chosen by the better colleges, or because in some ways, independent of talent, the degree from Harvard, Yale, or Columbia represents a credential that opens doors that lead to financial success (Kingston 1980). This point is especially worth noting because it contradicts the expressed view of some authors who believe that elite college graduates have a substantial edge in dealing with publishers. Coser, Kadushin, and Powell (1982) find that graduates of Ivy League and other elite schools are found in disproportionate numbers among publishers. Moreover, the same scholars suggest that some publishers appear attracted to academic authors at certain universities in part because of their institutional prestige. However, while some authors may have benefited from "old school ties," the proverbial distinction between Princeton and Podunk generally appears inconsequential in writing careers. The belief that an elite college degree represents an important advantage to financial success in writing is simply not supported by our data.

Geographic Location. Some might suppose that authors who live and work in the New York area, still the publishing capital of the United States, would do better financially than those elsewhere. Even if the social and professional connections among editors, agents, and writers are not as close as they are often portrayed (Coser, Kadushin, and Powell), the New York-based writers would seem to have relatively frequent access to the rounds of parties, lunches, and other get-togethers of the writing world which are often thought so significant for making deals.

We cannot say, on the basis of our survey, whether New York writers do in fact attempt more than others to promote their careers through these kinds of contacts. Yet whatever the case, where authors live and work has little to do with how much they earn from writing; most earn very little indeed. For example, 44 percent of the New York-based writers made less than $5,000 from writing in 1979 compared to 50 percent in California and 52 percent in the South. Perhaps more revealing is that, even among the small group of authors who earned upward of $50,000, no preponderance of New Yorkers appeared in that group. In fact, authors living in California turned up more often in this high-income group than those from any other region. Again, this aggregate analysis does not gainsay a possible effect on specific careers, but generally the "New York factor" is not of any notable consequence.

Race and Ethnicity. The racial and ethnic identities of individuals in American society are, among other factors, strongly related to their earned income.(See, e.g., Featherman and Hauser 1979, and Duncan, Featherman, and Duncan 1972.) Briefly, in 1980 black American males with full-time year round jobs had a median income of $13,875 compared to $19,720 among their white counterparts. Among women the respective figures were $10,915 and $11,703 (U.S. Bureau of the Census 1982). Regardless of educational achievement and background characteristics, there continues to be, as O. D. Duncan (1968) has noted, not only "inheritance of poverty" but also "inheritance of race." Racial prejudice and discrimination are still with us in the American occupation structure. Putting aside here questions of the various bases for the wage differentials between members of minorities and the majority, racial status continues to be a critical factor in explaining income in America.

How about within the writing profession? Altogether, just 2-3 percent of the authors in the sample classified themselves as black, Asian, Hispanic, or members of some other minority group. Given these small numbers, the results should be approached with caution. However, we find no prominent differences between their incomes and those of white authors. Twenty-three percent of the minority authors and 22 percent of the white authors earned more than $20,000 in 1979 from writing; on the other hand, 62 percent of the former and 50% of the latter earned less than $5,000.

Sex. Although women now constitute about 45 percent of the total labor force in American society, American women still earn far less from their jobs than similarly situated men. The ratio of female/male earnings of roughly .60 is the figure bandied around most frequently. This figure may create some distorted views because it does not reflect a variety of differences in the types of jobs that men and women typically hold (which may, in turn, partly reflect gender discrimination). Nonetheless, careful studies by economists and sociologists suggest that even after taking into account factors that might contribute to the gender difference (such as full-time vs. part-time jobs, education, type of jobs, and years of experience), women still earn substantially less, on average, than men in similar jobs. The earnings ratios obtained in these studies range typically from .60 to .93 (Lloyd and Niemi 1979). It is of some interest here that these ratios vary somewhat by type of occupation. The difference in male and female earnings is far less among scientists and other academics (.9 and higher) than in other occupations.

While income from writing is essentially unrelated to authors' social origins, educational achievements, and geographical location, it is not altogether free of social patterning. The general differences in income between men and women appear here, too, although such differences are comparatively muted. Female authors made up 40 percent of our total sample. Although we cannot be sure that this proportion exactly represented the ratio of females to males in the entire profession, or whether that ratio has changed significantly over, say, the past 100 years, it is plain that women today represent a very sizable portion of the overall community of freelance writers. These women authors earned a median of $4,000 from writing in 1979 compared to $5,200 earned by men. This ratio of .77, which does not take into account other factors that might explain the $1,200 difference, suggests a nontrivial difference and one which is undoubtedly consequential for writers themselves. Yet it is significantly smaller than the .60 ratio that characterizes the simple difference in the median incomes of men and women in the labor force generally.

That the income differences between men and women authors are relatively small is also shown by the fact that the chances of being in the bottom or the top income strata are unrelated to an author's sex. About the same proportions of men and women (37 percent as against 40 percent) earned less than $2,500 per year. Much the same situation holds at the other extreme of the income distribution: 10 percent of the men and 7 percent of the women made more than $50,000.[10] We also found no marked sex-related differences in income among those who work exclusively at writing, the committed full-timers who spent twenty-five hours a week or more at writing and had no other paid positions: 12 percent of the men and women in this group earned $20,000 or more.

When we consider the number of hours authors worked at writing, however, the ratio of female to male income varies significantly from the overall ratio of .77. In figure 4.4 we present in graphic form how both hours spent writing and sex influence writing income. For those authors who worked less than forty hours per week at writing, the gender differences in writing-related income were less than the overall ratio. For those working less than ten hours the female to male income ratio was .83, while it was .93 for writers working from ten to nineteen hours and .80 for those working twenty to thirty-nine hours. However, for men and women authors who worked at least forty hours each week at writing, the income returns to men were considerably higher than those of women. In this case, the ratio of female to male earnings was .56.

The differences between female and male earnings among the committed full-time authors were, in part, a result of the differences in the genres in which they worked. Children's books tend to yield lower incomes than other forms of writing (as indicated in table 4.7, below). Women were almost three times as likely as men to be primarily authors of children's books (25% against 9%).

Religious Background. Even a perfunctory review of the demographic composition of American authors leads to the conclusion that they are an exceptional lot, including their divergence from the larger population in religious composition. Authors with Jewish backgrounds represented almost one quarter of the total sample, compared with their approximate 4 percent in the American population. In fact, there were far more Jewish authors than Catholics, who represented 14 percent of the authors but roughly 37 percent of the U.S. population. Protestants, who constituted 40 percent of the authors, represented about 55 percent of the U.S. population.[11] The strong representation of Jews among authors conforms to the intuitive sense that they are well represented among the more renowned writers of contemporary fiction. Indeed, a subgenre of fiction during the 1950s, 60s, and 70s focused on aspects of Jewish life and experiences in America.

The high representation of Jewish writers should be only mildly surprising, since Jews tend to be strongly represented in most professional and highly skilled occupations, such as law, medicine,

Income

Figure 4.4. Time Commitment and Median Writing Income: A Comparison of Men and Women Authors

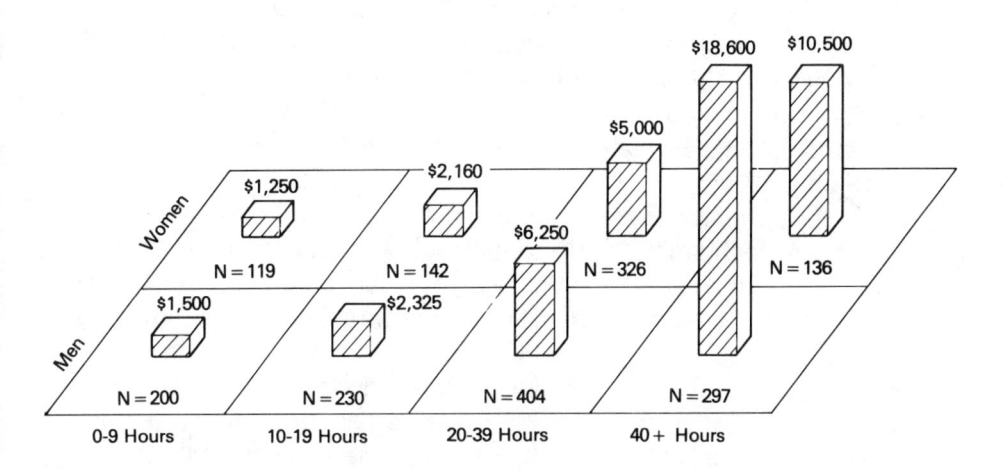

Women:
- 0-9 Hours: $1,250, N = 119
- 10-19 Hours: $2,160, N = 142
- 20-39 Hours: $5,000, N = 326
- 40+ Hours: $10,500, N = 136

Men:
- 0-9 Hours: $1,500, N = 200
- 10-19 Hours: $2,325, N = 230
- 20-39 Hours: $6,250, N = 404
- 40+ Hours: $18,600, N = 297

Hours Spent Writing Per Week

The number over each block represents the median 1979 writing-related income for that group. The n in each cell represents the number of authors on which the income block was computed.

and science. Indeed, Harriet Zuckerman (1977) showed in a study of elites in science that fully 27 percent of American Nobel Prize winners were Jewish. She went on to note that in American higher education, especially at the elite research universities, Jews were heavily represented among the professoriate. Furthermore, about a quarter of medical faculties had Jewish origins, a fact which underscores the longstanding attraction of the medical profession to American Jews.

While these proportions tell us something of the religious composition of the occupation, they tell us nothing about the relationship between religious origins and achievement. Past studies of this subject by Greeley (1976) and others suggest that Jews and most Catholic ethnic groups earn some 10-20 percent more than would be expected given their family economic background, education, and place of residence.

We ask, then; Is there any relationship between the religious background of authors and their subsequent earnings from their writings, and further, if differences exist, what can account for them? In fact, there are such differences. Authors with Catholic backgrounds earned more on average than authors from the other two major religious groups. Their 1979 median writing income was $6,000; their average was $24,780. In contrast, the median earnings in this year for Jewish authors was $5,650, or 94 percent of the earnings of Catholics; the average writing income for Jewish authors was $19,199. Protestant authors had significantly lower average and median incomes from writing: the figures were $4,125, or 69 percent of the incomes reported by Catholic authors, with an average of $17,814.[12]

What can we make of these differences? We certainly cannot look to the substance of the religions for any clues to why members of differing religious groups should earn different sums from their writing. If there is an answer to be found, then, it must be in features of writing activity or in backgrounds that are associated both with religious identification and with income. In fact, here we show that initial religious disparities in writing income partly reflect such relationships.

When we examine the income of authors in the three major religious groups in light of their type of commitment to writing,

Income

TABLE 4.5. The 1979 Writing-related Incomes (Medians) of Five Types of Authors with Different Religious Backgrounds

Religious background	Committed full-timers	Limited full-timers	Committed part-timers	Intermittent part-timers	Marginal part-timers
Roman Catholic	13,000 (264)	4,000 (51)	5,000 (41)	2,350 (51)	1,150 (28)
Jewish	18,000 (434)	4,080 (55)	4,000 (59)	3,000 (104)	1,225 (62)
Protestant	9,525 (726)	2,964 (147)	7,000 (84)	3,000 (153)	1,500 (100)

Note: The number of authors in each category represents the total for which we had both income and religious background information. We have excluded from the presentation the 96 authors who had "other" religious backgrounds and the 293 who claimed no religious background.

we find some marked shifts in the earnings ratios between religious groups. In table 4.5 we show the median 1979 earnings from writing for the five types of authors, classified by their religious background. Comparing committed full-time authors from Catholic and Jewish backgrounds, we found a reversal in the difference: a median 1979 writing income of $18,000 for Jewish authors compared with $13,000 for Roman Catholics, or an earnings ratio of 1.38. The difference between Protestants and Catholics was slightly reduced: the ratio of earnings was .73 among these full-timers. For the other types of authors except intermittent part-timers, Jewish writers earned more than their Catholic counterparts. Furthermore, among each type of part-time author, the Protestants had the highest median incomes. So, at least part of the overall difference in incomes among religious groups can be explained by their somewhat differing representation among the several types of authors, and the pattern of religious disparity varies greatly among the types.

For this reason, differences in productivity also warrant attention. Among authors who have published at least ten books in their careers, we found that Jewish authors earned virtually the same as Catholics (.98 ratio), but differences in earnings between Catholic and Protestant authors remained substantial (.60 ratio).[13] Within the range of five to nine published books, Jewish authors had somewhat higher median incomes than Catholics, but Protestants still lagged behind both. With authors of three or four books we found that both Jewish and Protestant writers had median incomes of slightly less than half that of Catholics.

This complex pattern of results does not have any obvious explanation, but does again suggest that the overall religious disparity does not fully reflect the experiences of specific groups of authors. Relatedly, we also found that differences in the sex compositon of the religious groups accounted for part of their income disparities, and the pattern of religious disparities varied by educational level.

The same may be said about the genre in which authors work.[14] Among the authors of adult nonfiction and children's books, Jewish authors made on average more than their Catholic counterparts who, in turn, made more than Protestants. However, among those writing genre fiction, the Catholics enjoyed the greatest average success, and the Protestants had the highest earnings of the academically oriented writers. In still yet another pattern, the Catholic and Jewish authors of adult fiction had similar average incomes, substantially more than Protestant authors in this genre. These differences among the various genres cannot be explained by these data, but they indicate that no religious group has a distinctive, general "talent" for making money from writing.

Before closing this discussion of writing incomes and religious background, two points should be reiterated. First, the median incomes for all these subgroups tended to be small, so that relatively small absolute differences in median incomes produce rather large ratio differences in earnings. Second, the variance within each religious group in the economic return to writing was far greater than the difference among religious groups. There is, in short, a marked overlap in the incomes of members of all these religious groups, despite the existence of differences in their median writing-related incomes.

Summarizing the Effects of Personal Characteristics. Briefly, the results from the survey plainly indicate that personal and social background has a very slight effect on chances of financial success in writing. There is no "right" or preferred social origin or background that significantly enhances an author's economic prospects. In statistical terms, the combination of these personal and social characteristics, including parents' education, father's occupation, race (white, nonwhite), gender, religious background, and whether the author had a close relative with a published book accounted for only 1 percent of the total variation in authors' 1979 writing income.

CAREER HISTORY

So much for the relationships between author's incomes and their social and personal characteristics. Are there more compelling linkages between writing incomes and certain attributes of author's writing careers such as their publication histories, the sorts of writing they do, and the critical notice their work receives?

As a first step in answering this question, let us consider how a very crude "human capital" model applies to the distibution of writing incomes. Many economists (see, among many others, Becker 1964, Mincer 1974) have stressed the importance of formal education and job experience for enhancing productivity. On the further assumption that workers are paid in accord with their marginal productivity, those relatively well endowed with human capital—the well educated and experienced—should be relatively well rewarded. Countless empirical investigations have revealed this to be so. Of course, as economists recognize, productivity is an elusive concept and its determinants are not always well understood. This is certainly so for writing, a largely unroutinized activity, calling for unusual, often creative skills. Its "product" is economically rewarded in light of diverse commercial-aesthetic judgments.

It is not greatly surprising, then, that regression models incorporating only measures of education and job experience explain no variance in writing income. Here, "job experience" is crudely measured by length of time from first book publication to the present.[15] In short, there is no detectable economic payoff in this occupation to job experience or the job training which formal schooling provides.

To be sure, no one seriously entertains the idea that schooling per se consistently produces more economically successful writers—that commercial success in writing is a directly teachable skill as, say, architectural drafting. And, similarly, no one really believes that the experienced writers, simply by virtue of long years at the typewriter, regularly acquire writing skills which are translated into higher sales. Yet the fact that these human capital variables, which do so well in predicting earnings in other occupations, provide no understanding of how the economic rewards are distributed among authors underscores a distinctive aspect of the writing enterprise.

Publication Histories. However, again not surprisingly, a direct measure of productivity—number of published books—does appear to count financially.

Among recently published authors (1977–1980), the number of prior publications was significantly related to income from writing in 1979 (see table 4.6). Of the authors who had no more than two published books to their credit, the relatively silent author, almost half (43 %) had incomes lower than $2,500. By contrast, only 12 percent of prolific authors, those with ten or more books published, had such low incomes. Correlatively, more than twice the proportion of prolific authors earned more than $20,000 from writing in 1979 as those who had published just one or two books. All this is expectable. The more authors continue to publish, the more apt they are to earn royalties and to get favorable royalty arrangements from publishers. This holds in general in spite of the conspicuous case of certain one-book authors whose contracts, royalties, and subsidiary rights have received copious attention from the press.

Generally, however, even prolific authors must continue to publish if they wish to avoid substantial drops in income over the short run. For example, 58 percent of the prolific authors (a total of ten or more books published) who had failed to publish in the preceding three years earned less than $5,000 from their writing in 1979 in contrast to 21 percent of equally prolific authors who were published so recently. At higher income levels, we found that among prolific authors, 39 percent of the recently published compared with 11 percent who had not published recently earned $20,000 or more from writing in 1979.

Types of Books. Of course, authors do not produce an undifferentiated "product." Authors, agents, and publishers are all apt to

TABLE 4.6. Publishing Productivity and 1979 Writing Income

Number of Books Published (year of last book publication)

	1977–1980					1970–1976			
Writing income	10+	5–9	3–4	0–2		10+	5–9	3–4	0–2
$0–2,499	12	23	29	43		43	53	53	73
$2,500–4,999	9	17	17	16		15	13	9	8
$5,000–9,999	19	15	21	13		15	15	13	4
$10,000–19,999	21	17	10	11		17	13	9	6
$20,000–49,999	25	17	14	10		9	6	9	7
$50,000–99,999	7	7	6	4		2	1	6	2
$100,000+	7	4	4	3		—	—	1	1
Total (rounded)	100%	100%	101%	100%		101%	101%	100%	101%
	(359)	(303)	(248)	(297)		(47)	(72)	(87)	(138)

have strong convictions about the kinds of books that make the most money. Poets and academics writing for specialists, for instance, do not have to be told that their prospects for a "blockbuster" are slight, but systematic data on the relationship between genre and income have been missing.

To get some sense of how these matters stand, we devised a classification of book genres to reflect types of book markets rather than aesthetic judgments. Authors were asked to choose a single category (among eleven choices; see column headings of table 4.7) to which they had committed the most time in their writing careers. This represents a limitation of the data because many authors report dividing their time between and even among genres.

Before turning to the matter of money, we note that authors most commonly described themselves as writers of adult nonfiction (26%), with substantial numbers involved in general adult fiction (19%), children's books (15%), genre fiction, i.e., westerns, thrillers, science fiction, historical romances, and gothic/occult novels (13%), and academically oriented nonfiction (12%).

As the preceding section suggested, recentness of publication is notably related to writing income. Accordingly, in table 4.7 we restrict analysis to authors who have been published between 1977 and 1980. Obviously in certain categories there are too few cases for valid inference, but the distributions relating to these categories are at least suggestive. Observe also that to focus on the specific economic impact of writing genre, table 4.7 classifies *book* writing-related income, not the somewhat more inclusive measure of writing-related income. However, for most authors these figures are virtually identical.

Above all, what this table indicates is a general pattern of low financial returns from book authorship across all genres, but particular variations are of interest. With the single exception of genre fiction writers, about half of the authors in each category—and in some cases considerably more—earned less than $5,000 in 1979. And, in fact, the largest number within each genre received less than $2,500. Still, the genre fiction writers were relatively successful: almost a quarter earned in excess of $50,000. By comparison, 15 percent of the general adult fiction writers, 8 percent of the general nonfiction authors, and 7 percent of the children's writers reached this level. (The

TABLE 4.7. How Much Authors in Various Genres Earned from Book Writing in 1979

Genre

1979 Writing income	Genre fiction	General adult fiction	Academically oriented nonfiction	Adult nonfiction	How-to books	Technical reports Manuals/ textbooks	Poetry	Children's books	Religious/ inspirational	Translations	Other	Total
$0–2,499	17	29	54	34	37	38	59	23	25	60	46	33 (379)
$2,500–4,999	10	16	14	13	12	15	14	18	17	0	13	14 (162)
$5000–9,999	15	10	14	15	21	10	9	21	8	20	17	15 (177)
$10,000–19,999	12	13	10	18	21	15	9	18	17	0	17	15 (175)
$20,000–49,999	21	18	7	13	7	18	9	12	17	0	8	13 (160)
$50,000–99,999	13	9	0	6	1	3	0	4	8	20	0	6 (68)
$100,000+	10	6	1	2	1	3	0	3	8	0	0	3 (42)
Total (rounded)	98%	101%	100%	101%	100%	102%	100%	99%	100%	100%	101%	99%
	(149)	(207)	(138)	(302)	(68)	(40)	(22)	(196)	(12)	(5)	(24)	(1,163)

Note: Only recently published authors (1977–1980) are included in this table.

virtual exclusion of "how-to" authors from the top income brackets is perhaps surprising given the profusion of best sellers on how to run, eat, dress, cope, and so forth. However, these authors may have considered themselves part of the adult nonfiction category.)

The writers of children's books fared somewhat worse than the writers of general adult fiction and nonfiction. The children's book authors slightly exceeded their adult book counterparts in the likelihood of at least earning more than $5,000, but they were less likely to reach the $20,000 mark. The contrast with adult fiction writers was quite sharp: 19 percent of the children's book authors earned more than $20,000 as compared to 33 percent of the adult fiction writers.

To see the economic return of various genres in another light, consider the results presented in figure 4.5, which shows median 1979 writing-related income in terms of a cross-classification of genre and time commitment to writing. (Only the four most common genres are considered.) There are two important results here. First, for each category of time commitment, some differences appear in median income figures among the genres, and this is particularly notable among authors who reported working at least forty hours a week at writing. Second, and perhaps more striking, is that within each genre authors writing less than forty hours a week typically earned very little from writing. Within each genre the authors who spent at least forty hours a week at writing-related work were typically much more successful than their counterparts who spent fewer hours engaged in literary activities. With a median writing-related income of $31,500, the genre fiction writers who put in at least forty hours a week were clearly the most successful group.

Critical Notice, Honorific Recognition, and Income. Just as members of the publishing community have strong convictions about the types of books that are apt to sell well, so many publishers and authors are also convinced that a book must be reviewed in an important place to have any prospects of financial success and that winning a prestigious book award is a great financial boon.

Thus, one editor-in-chief of a publishing house recently remarked: "I greatly welcome a review in the *Times* no matter whether it is favorable or not; any review [in the *New York Times*] sells books."[16]

Income

Figure 4.5: Time Commitment and Median Income: A Comparison of Genres

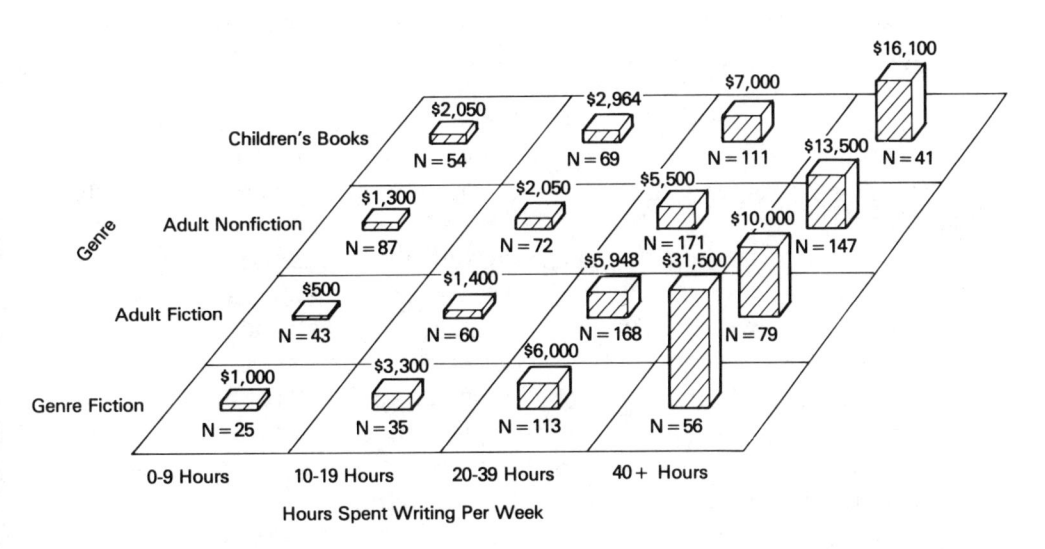

Children's Books:
- 0-9 Hours: —
- 10-19 Hours: $2,050, N=54
- 20-39 Hours: $2,964, N=69
- 40+ Hours: $7,000, N=111; $16,100, N=41

Adult Nonfiction:
- 0-9 Hours: $1,300, N=87
- 10-19 Hours: $2,050, N=72
- 20-39 Hours: $5,500, N=171; $10,000, N=147
- 40+ Hours: $13,500

Adult Fiction:
- 0-9 Hours: $500, N=43
- 10-19 Hours: $1,400, N=60
- 20-39 Hours: $5,948, N=168
- 40+ Hours: $31,500, N=79

Genre Fiction:
- 0-9 Hours: $1,000, N=25
- 10-19 Hours: $3,300, N=35
- 20-39 Hours: $6,000, N=113
- 40+ Hours: N=56

Hours Spent Writing Per Week

The number over each block represents the median 1979 writing-related income for that group. The n in each cell represents the number of authors on which the income block was computed.

But while a *Times* review seems to have special prominence, not all observers believe that a review in that publication or any other is decisive or even consistently consequential for a book's sales.

On the basis of the information at hand, we cannot say whether the frequency with which authors' books are reviewed is related to their financial return, nor can we say whether good reviews count more than bad ones. We can report that the authors in our sample whose recent books have been reviewed in the *New York Times Book Review* did better financially than those the *Times* passed by. Forty-one percent of authors whose books were reviewed in this one publication earned $20,000 or more in 1979 compared with 20 percent of those not reviewed there. But being reviewed has little relation to earning a respectable income from writing: 44 percent of the authors whose books were reviewed in the *Times* earned less than $10,000 in 1979.

Findings like these are difficult to interpret. To conclude that prominent critical notice itself enhances authors' incomes is plainly unwarranted. In some measure, authors' prior literary and financial success affects their chances of being reviewed; authors with a "track record" are more likely to receive attention. For these authors, critical attention may as much reflect past success as create new prospects. And in some measure, the literary merits of some prominently reviewed books may be rewarded in the marketplace for entirely other reasons. In the absence of the sorts of data needed to understand the reciprocal influences within these complex relationships, all we can say is that being reviewed in the *Times* is correlated but may not be the cause of greater writing income.

Such data on the correlation between critical notice and authors' incomes are at least consistent with some prevailing wisdom. However, the findings we now report on authors' incomes and literary awards may contravene some of this wisdom. First note that throughout their careers the majority of authors (54%) have received no awards, or even nominations for awards, for their writing. Eighteen percent had received or had been nominated for one award, 13 percent for two, and 15 percent for three or more.

What is striking is that among the recently published writers (1977–1980), there were only quite modest differences in the

Income

writing incomes of award winners and those not honored for their work. To detail, just more than half (51%) of the nonhonored writers received less than $5,000 from book writing, while 42 percent of the award winners also suffered this fate. Nor were the award winners distinctly likely to reap substantial success: 7 percent of the nonhonored and 10 percent of the honored earned more than $50,000. And, indeed, of the frequently honored (three or more awards), only a small minority of 13 percent reached this income level. Of course, these figures indicate that the frequently honored have slightly less than twice the chance of earning $50,000 as the nonhonored, though the low probability for both remains unmistakably clear.

But all awards are not of a piece. Some carry great prestige and publicity, others are less significant and bring little attention. Drawing upon the advice of the members of the Authors Guild Advisory Board, we divided the awards listed by authors into two classes, major and minor, and proceeded to examine the incomes of winners of these two classes of awards.[17]

Winners of major awards earned somewhat more than winners of minor ones, but prestigious honors were not typically accompanied by great financial reward. Among the recently published authors (1977–1980), 29 percent of the major and 45 percent of the minor award winners earned less than $5,000 from their book writing. But if a major reward reduced chances of impoverishment from writing, it did little to enhance chances of material comforts. Almost half received less than $10,000 from writing, and only 14 percent of the prestigiously honored earned in excess of $50,000, a rate not much higher than that among the winners of lesser awards (10%).

As table 4.4 above indicates, the bivariate relationship between a measure of honorific recognition (no award, minor award, and major award) and (log of) writing income is .15. This association is quite modest, but it is notable given the general low level of patterning in the distribution of writing income. Moreover, multivariate analyses (discussed on pp. 91–92 and in appendix C) indicate that this measure has some slight effect on (the log of) income independent of a number of writing career–related factors. (It is not independently related to untransformed income.)

This brief analysis of formal recognition necessarily relies on gross categorizations (numbers of awards and a major-minor distinction) and does not gainsay the fact that particular awards may be crucial to the economic fortunes of certain authors at certain points in their careers. Nevertheless, the very modest associations revealed here suggest that there is at best a loose coupling between honorific and economic rewards for authors.

Publishing Houses. While complaints among authors about publishers are legion, there appears to be a widespread belief that the larger houses are at least relatively successful in generating sales—to be sure, from the typical author's viewpoint, never as successfully as his or her book deserves. And publishers at the larger houses undoubtedly assert this advantage in attempting to sell their house to authors.

The data indicate that there is some support for this view, though the implications of the findings are not altogether clear. Among recently published authors (1977–1980), those whose most recent book was published by a "major" house had somewhat higher 1979 book-related incomes than those published by a less prominent house.[18] Some 13 percent of those published by a major house earned in excess of $50,000 compared to 5 percent of those published by other houses. Not only were those published by a major house more likely to be found within the upper income brackets, but they were also less likely to have fared poorly. The 40 percent who earned less than $5,000 could hardly be cheered by their economic fortunes, but 53 percent of the others had to endure this condition. While those published by a major house have some edge over the others, the fact remains that the overwhelming majority must contend with very modest or low incomes, whoever the publisher.

Of course, like the impact of a track record or a *Times* review, it is impossible to determine whether this edge reflects the effects of a house's stature per se. "Marketable" writers may simply be relatively attracted to the major houses. And, while more talented and saleable writers may be selected by the major houses, we cannot say that their promotional efforts lead to greater sales than would occur at smaller houses. Plainly, the relationship between a publishing house's stature and the characteristics of an author's writing is a complex one that should not be interpreted causally.

CAREER FACTORS: VARIATION IN WRITING INCOME

To provide more differentiated information on how authors of varying personal and career characteristics fare economically by writing, we have concentrated on simple bivariate relationships. Our primary effort has been to detail the actual distributions of writing income among those with different personal backgrounds, occupational commitments, and experiences in their writing careers. As the statistically informed reader readily recognizes, we have made very little systematic effort to explain variance or estimate the "net effect" of various factors on writing income. Such analysis essentially involves an exercise in attempting to find and understand patterns among very small differences. Some brief reference to the results of limited multivariate analyses may nonetheless help us summarize our findings.

Even without more sophisticated multivariate analysis, it is quite apparent that social background characteristics can explain very little variance in writing income. As we noted, multiple regression models incorporating measures of parental education and occupation (including background as an author), race, sex, and religion can explain less than 1 percent of the variance.

Yet our analyses do suggest that certain career factors and writing commitments are at least modestly related to writing income. We therefore ran multiple regression models of 1979 writing income (and various transformations of this figure) on average number of hours a week spent writing; whether the author wrote full-time; recency of publication; number of books published; primary genre of the author; and extent of honorific recognition. We refer interested readers to appendix C for details on variable measurement and model specifications as well as the statistical results.

Here we may simply relate that, in order, the three strongest predictors of an author's writing income (more precisely, the log of income) are recency of publication, hours per week writing, and number of books produced. By comparison, the effect of honorific recognition is slight, and full-time status as well as genre do not have a significant effect. Together, all the variables in our model account for a quarter of the variance in (the log of) writing income.[19]

The results corroborate what we have previously asserted: recently published, prolific authors who manage to commit long hours to writing tend to do relatively well. And yet knowing these things about an author's writing commitment and career provides only a very partial understanding of his economic standing.

Success Within Occupational Groups: Authorship as an Unusual Case

Throughout the preceding discussion we have noted that the occupation of author is unusual in several ways. Here we highlight some of these distinctive features and offer some theoretical explanation for them.

As we have pointed out, an ever-increasing number of studies by both economists and sociologists document that within the labor force experience and training pay off, that is, human capital is economically rewarded; and a more limited set of studies indicates that this is also true within specific occupations and labor markets.[20] Thus we expect to find *ceteris paribus* that more experienced factory workers, policemen, accountants, or business executives earn more than their less experienced counterparts. Similarly we expect relatively well-educated teachers, computer programmers, and government bureaucrats to have relatively high earnings. And yet, as we have demonstrated, education and experience apparently have no direct payoff for authors. Our analysis does not show that writing skill, including a feel for and ability to produce what is sellable goes economically unrewarded, but it does show that those factors—experience and schooling—which are commonly viewed as proxies for (or direct contributions to) job-specific skills are of little consequence in explaining variation in writing income.

The unusual situation of authors is further underscored by the fact that patterns of success seem unrelated, or only weakly related, to social factors that are generally good predictors of success, such as family economic status, race, sex, and the "cultural capital" or social polish acquired from attending elite schools. These ascribed factors provide very little economic edge among authors, though abundant evidence exists that within the work force as a whole, and in many specific occupations and labor markets, "who you are" or "what you are" are critical determinants of success.

There are, of course, good reasons for us not to expect either experience or levels of educational achievement to affect the financial returns to authors from their writing. After all, writing ability is not something which can be reduced to teachable skills and "tricks of the trade," conveyed in some education program like accounting. More than that, even though skills may be honed through practice, experience per se— the actual number of years pounding on a typewriter—does not necessarily make a writer better or more marketable. Some writers just seem to have more talent than others, and dogged effort alone should not be expected to compensate for these differences.

Additionally, no one seriously believes—certainly not most authors themselves—that writing skill, much less literary or intellectual merit, is rewarded in the marketplace. The skilled poet, for instance, knows that he will not receive much financial recompense, no matter what the quality of his work. Poets do not make money by writing poetry, and everyone knows that; in effect, they are choosing not to succeed financially. They and other authors are not motivated primarily by money.

Authors are, of course, not alone in this ordering of priorities. Scholars of the performing artists have found much the same pattern. For example, in her study of dancers, Fredricka Santos first notes that "in 1960, the observed mean net income of male dancers and dance teachers ($4,384) was 7 percent less than that of high school graduates ($4,733)" (1976: 254). In concluding, she reinforces what we have found for authors: The data

do plead the precariousness of professional life in the performing arts and the financial sacrifice inherent. For both dancers and singers, the observed percentage differentials were never as large as the estimated differentials required to compensate the respective groups for their investment.... Risk preference and psychic income apparently prevail over financial considerations when considering the pursuit of a career in the performing arts. (p. 257)

Even for authors who direct their efforts to writing genres offering some prospect of financial success, the connection between any reasonable sense of talent or skill and financial success seems at most very loose. Some writers may be more able to respond to the reading public's demand than others, but it is difficult to portray this responsiveness as any definable skill. Also, the public appeal of a book is not determined by its intrinsic qualities alone; the significance of promotional efforts cannot be overlooked. Furthermore, less tangible qualities among authors may have some significant effect on financial success. Some writers are simply better entrepreneurs than others; some can advertise themselves more sucessfully.

That social demographic factors account for so little of the differences in income derived from writing also makes sense. Whatever their ambivalences about appearing commercial, publishers want to make money on their books. Certainly they have no incentive to sabotage the financial returns to their writers because of the authors' demographic traits. They may underpromote a book, but it is unlikely to be done because the author has a limited education. Nor are they apt to publish the works of certain types of authors in the first place if they believe that social characteristics of authors per se may depress sales. Publication itself implies the belief that there is a market for the book. And, in general, it may be presumed that self-interest leads publishers to believe that the work has relatively good chances of generating sales within the particular market niche at which it is aimed, that it has a life of its own in the marketplace which is not systematically affected by the social characteristics of the author. To the extent that there is discrimination in how different types of authors are treated in the publishing industry, the great part of it probably involves the publication decision, not subsequent dealings. This does not mean, of course, that publishers are not guilty of creating self-fulfilling prophecies in estimating the sales of authors' books. Undoubtedly they do set up conditions for this prophecy by linking expected sales to marketing efforts. However, there is no reason to believe that those market decisions are correlated with the social characteristics of authors' backgrounds.

Together, these considerations suggest that the financial rewards from writing should not be influenced by the same factors that govern financial success in other occupations. The occupation author is clearly different—in the nature of its product, in the organization of the work process, and in the diverse and often unusual motivation of those who write. Indeed, a relatively low level of social patterning in the distribution of economic rewards appears as one of the most notable characteristics of the occupation.

THEORETICAL CONSIDERATIONS

The various distinct features of the occupation are worth noting in themselves, but a larger analytical point arises. What general features of occupations—and, concomitantly, markets in which they are embedded—account for the type and extent of social patterning of intraoccupational attainment? Theoretical frameworks and relevant empirical studies that address this question are at best scanty. And it certainly is not our purpose here to articulate a theory of intraoccupational attainment. However, consideration of the economic condition of authors, along with other works on related subjects, suggest some elements which might be incorporated into such a theory.

Here we consider first the extent to which the occupation is embedded in an "internal labor market"; second, whether some status group "controls" the occupation; third, whether the skills necessary for job performance have been standardized; and fourth, whether the psychological motivations of those entering the occupation comport with the drives of "economic man," the maximizer of economically rooted utility.

First of all, the occupation of author exhibits characteristics which are almost the polar opposites of those occupations in which there exists an internal labor market. Such a market is characterized, as Doeringer and Piore (1971) suggest, by well-defined ports of entry, formal regulations related to hiring and promotion, and explicit career ladders which all with aspirations for advancement must climb. These features tend to insulate the distribution of rewards within an occupation from the competitive pressures of the larger (external) labor market. They thereby enhance the importance of administrative rules and procedures, which generally tend to stress criteria involving standardized measures of experience (years on the job) and educational certification. For example, Grandjean's (1981) analysis of white-collar workers in the federal bureaucracy, perhaps an exemplar of an internal market with highly specified promotion paths and procedures, showed that education and age alone were powerful predictors of salary for these workers, much more so than for the general population of employed workers.[21] We should expect, then, that human capital variables have relatively pronounced effects in occupations with internal labor markets, such as the professions of law and medicine, certain construction and other blue-collar crafts, and managerial administrative positions (especially those in the large corporate and governmental sectors of the economy).

Consider how authors lack any connection to an internal labor market. Anyone can enter the occupation; there is no designated port of entry. There is no specified career ladder to climb; for the most part, authors are only as good as their most recent book, and no consistent upward pattern results from that. Obviously, there are no regulations governing career advancement for authors; publishers and the reading public alike are more interested in the product than the process by which it is produced. And this product is usually created alone—whether in the fabled garret or the plushly appointed study—largely removed from the constraints of any organizational structure. With these characteristics, one should expect, as we indeed find, that the financial success of authors is relatively unaffected by job experience and education. For the same reasons we find similar low returns to human capital within other artistic and entertainment-related occupations (Baumol and Bowen 1966; Bowen and Finegan 1969; Blaug 1976.)

A second factor to consider is the extent of status group control of an occupation. Whether education is predominantly rewarded *because* it enhances productivity, as human capital theory suggests, is a matter we cannot settle here. But, at minimum, some analyses cast doubt on this contention and direct attention to the political side of the occupational world. It has been argued that much of the increasing importance of education in careers may be attributed to the attempt of certain groups to enhance their postion by imposing educational requirements for jobs which they seek to make their own (Collins 1979). These educational requirements thus serve to screen out the competitors and favor that group which has dominated the occupation. Indirectly, then, social background characteristics influence promotion within the occupation.Therefore, educational requirements, including informal considerations of degree prestige, should be relatively pronounced for top-level corporate managers, and the proper educational-social pedigree may be almost necessary to enter a top Wall Street firm.

Again, in this light, the muted effects of background characteristics on the financial success of authors are understandable. No particular status group (or groups) has controlled the occupation or is in a position to impose training requirements which indirectly benefit their group or to discriminate in favor of their own group more directly. To be sure, as Coser, Kadushin, and Powell (1982) have aptly noted, there is an " asymmetry of power" between authors and publishers, but this latter occupational group has no incentive to impose its social organization on authors.

A third factor to consider is simply the nature of the skills involved in getting the job done. When the skill involved in a task (such as writing commercially) is relatively rare and even idiosyncratic, not readily reducible to a training regimen, and not subject to clear a priori standards of merit, the occupation which emerges seems unlikely to have met much coherent structure. By sharp contrast, the skills involved in actuarial science, for example, are definable and teachable. They also seem to be systematically enhanced through job experience and may be consistently evaluated. The technology involved in this and similar tasks, then, seems at least relatively amenable to a socially organized occupational form.

Furthermore, we must consider the dispositions and motivations of those who enter an occupation. It is probably a tolerable simplification of life to presume, as do most economists, that individuals act to maximize their utility, which usually translates into a concern for economic reward. Thus, individuals should be expected to move into occupations in which their own particular endowments of human capital have the highest expected return.

But if that is the typical pattern, it is not necessarily the universal one. Surely, the desire to be an author or to pursue any of the performing arts would seem to confound this expectation because the expected rewards are generally so meager. As Santos has noted, however, "The predisposition to enter what may be diagnosed as a professional disaster area" may be attributed to "unfounded optimism, ignorance of the odds," or perhaps most aptly, to a risk-taking propensity (1976:243). Whatever the case, these unusual dispositions should tend to upset the "usual relationships" between individual characteristics and financial reward. Also, insofar as individuals pursue an occupation for *non*financial rewards—the psychic gratifications of a well-crafted, critically applauded volume of poetry, say, or an artful classical dance—we may further expect the usual relationships not to hold.

In a preliminary way, then, we are arguing that the social organization of an occupation, conditioned by the skill and technology involved in performing a task, as well as the motivations of the workers largely affect what factors are important in explaining intraoccupational success. Given the extreme lack of coherent structure in the writing profession, no doubt fostered by the unusual nature of its product and its practitioners, the relative absence of social patterning in the distribution of financial rewards among authors makes sense.

While human capital variables that influence earnings in the general labor force do not seem to have equivalent effects for predicting authors' writing-related earnings, education and experience should be expected to play a significant role in determining the income of authors generated from sources other than their writing. The nonwriting employment opportunities that enable authors to make ends meet are in fact dependent on both their educational background and their experience as writers. In short, human capital factors may play a more important role in predicting the overall personal incomes of authors than their writing-related incomes. And, indeed, as expected authors generally do well.

Total Personal and Family Income

By any estimation, most authors could not begin to support themselves by their freelance writing, and as we indicated in chapter 3, the large majority seek income from other jobs or fee-for-service writing-related activities for that very reason. Our survey indicates, however, that authors are generally able to subsidize their writing at a substantial level.

Authors reported median personal incomes from all sources of $27,000 in 1979, of which, it will be remembered, typically $4,800 came from writing (see table 4.8). This summary figure, which includes both earned and unearned income, conceals considerable variation.[22] In 1979, for example, the bottom quarter authors earned less than $13,000 from all sources, while the top quarter earned more than $45,000. At the extremes of the distribution of personal income, the lowest tenth made less than $5,000 and the highest tenth, almost $80,000.

We reported that, as expected, full-time authors earned more from writing than part-time authors. When it came to total personal income, however, the financial positions of these two groups were sharply reversed. Full-time authors in effect pay a price for their commitment to writing. In 1979, part-time authors earned median personal incomes of $30,000—one and a half times as much as the personal incomes of full time authors.

For comparison, we note here that the median personal income of $27,000 among authors exceeded that of salaried professional-technical workers ($18,164) and managers-administrators ($20,055), yet was slightly below that of self-employed professional-technical workers ($29,357) (U.S. Bureau of the Census 1980).

SALARIES FROM OTHER JOBS

The personal incomes of the part-timers reflect, of course, salaries from other well-paying jobs. The median salary among the

TABLE 4.8. The 1979 Total Personal Income of Five Author Types: Medians and Distributional Measures on Income; Median Ratios of Writing Income to Total Personal Income

Income	Total sample of authors	Committed full-timers	Limited full-timers	Committed part-timers	Intermittent part-timers	Marginal part-timers
Median	$27000	$24,000	$19,000	$29,650	$31,425	$30,825
90%	78,720	95,000	66,700	75,503	72,710	74,750
75%	45,000	45,988	36,000	46,875	46,750	48,000
25%	13,000	10,031	8,020	15,368	18,888	21,000
10%	5,000	3,500	3,941	7,288	8,000	9,525
N	1903	628	319	236	396	244
Median ratio of writing income to total personal income	.33	.77	.29	.26	.10	.05
N		595	294	226	377	221

Income

marginal part-time authors was $25,000; among the intermittent authors, $24,000; and among the committed, $12,000.

The success of authors in the larger occupational world, it bears repeating, is not surprising. For one thing, having completed a median of almost sixteen years of schooling as compared with the 12.4 completed by Americans generally, they are far better educated than most of the adult population. They are thus abundantly endowed with human capital, and most authors with other jobs hold some kind of managerial or professional position.

These salaries almost always represent a large proportion of the part-timer's personal income. Among the intermittent and marginal part-timers, the median contribution was about 80 cents of every dollar, and for a quarter of these authors more than 90 cents came from their salaries. Because of the relatively great amount of time they give to writing, the committed part-timers generally received proportionately less from their salaries. About half of the personal income of committed part-timers typically came from salaried employment.

INVESTMENTS, PENSIONS, AND SOCIAL SECURITY

In general, neither full-time nor part-time authors received much from "investments/pensions/Social Security." Although some authors have inherited private means, writers are not a monied lot. The median level of income derived from investments, pensions, and Social Security—a category which encompasses much more than inherited money—was $1,200. While the full-timers generally received somewhat more than the part-timers, no type of author received much from these sources. However, a tenth of the full-timers received more than $25,000, and a similar proportion of the part-timers got more than $15,000 from them. In all probability, the lion's share of these amounts came from pensions, Social Security, and interest returns on the author's own investments. The wording of the question does not allow us to specify the exact sources of this total.

These sources typically represented about 5 percent of authors' personal incomes. They assumed major significance—85 percent of total personal income—for only a tenth of all authors.[23]

PROPORTIONAL CONTRIBUTION OF WRITING INCOME
TO PERSONAL INCOME

Writing income typically represented less than half of a writer's personal income. Even if we add "total income directly related to writing" and "income from other freelance writing work" to create a broad definition of writing income, the representative author made only one-third of his or her personal income from writing.[24] Nonetheless, as we have come to anticipate, there were substantial variations in this proportion among our five types of authors (see table 4.8 above). Writing income accounted for the great part (77%) of the representative committed full-timers' personal income; but the median level among limited full-timers was only 29 percent. The median level among the committed part-timers was 26 percent, and for the intermittent and marginal part-timers writing income meant relatively little (a median level of 10 percent and 5 percent, respectively). Less than one in four of these intermittent and marginal part-timers earned even a quarter of their personal income from writing.

FAMILY INCOME

For the unmarried, personal and family income are the same, but for the married it is the combined total of personal and spouse's income that determines one's level of economic well-being. We therefore report the authors' total family income, an aggregate measure of all earned and unearned income, including a spouse's.[25]

Table 4.9 indicates how authors fared in terms of family income. The median total family income reached $38,000. Three-quarters of the authors had family incomes of at least $22,850, and a tenth had a total family income of less than $12,120. It is worth emphasizing, however, that a full-time commitment to writing in effect imposes an income penalty. The median total family income for each type of part-time author was in the $40,000 range, while the full-timers received about $5,000 less.

To place authors' total family incomes in perspective, we can show how they compared with quintile total income rankings of families within the American population—that is, what percentage of the authors had family incomes that placed them in the top fifth,

TABLE 4.9. The 1979 Total Family Income by Five Author Types: Median and Distributional Measures of Income: Median Ratios of Writing Income to Total Family Income

Five Types of Authors

Family income	Total sample of authors	Committed full-timers	Limited full-timers	Committed part-timers	Intermittent part-timers	Marginal part-timers
Median	$38,000	$35,050	$35,000	$39,800	$40,400	$41,500
90%	100,000	111,650	98,110	104,500	92,808	92,750
75%	60,500	62,225	58,850	61,000	57,025	60,000
25%	22,850	20,001	19,000	27,050	26,630	27,900
10%	12,120	10,000	8,843	15,084	16,480	18,450
N	1871	624	315	233	387	238
Median Ratio of Writing Income to Total Family Income	.14	.49	.12	.16	.07	.03
N		601	294	222	374	225

second fifth, etc., of the national income distribution (U.S. Bureau of the Census 1980). It turns out that more than 60 percent of the authors were in the top fifth of the national income distribution; 35 percent were in the top 5 percent. By contrast, less than 15 percent were in the lowest two-fifths of the distribution.

Of course, such a highly educated group should be expected to do well relative to the general population. Yet even if we limit the comparison to families where the head of household has at least a college degree, we find that the 1979 median total family income of $38,000 among authors exceeded by about 40 percent the national mean household income headed by a college-educated person. Their family incomes, then, fell considerably short of elite professionals and executives, though they exceeded those of the college-educated populace which generally holds managerial and professional jobs.

Proportional Contribution of Writing to Family Income. If writing income generally represents a small part of authors' personal incomes, it obviously plays an even smaller role in affecting the material comforts of authors' families. Indeed, an author's total writing income—again defined as "total income related to writing" and "income from other freelance writing work"—typically represented only 14 percent of his or her total family income. Even the committed full-timers typically made slightly less than half of their total family income through writing, which was a far greater proportion than for the other author types (see table 4.9). Not even a quarter of the other types earned half of their total family income by writing.

In short, while the great majority of authors live reasonably well, few of their families count on writing income to produce the means of achieving this well-being.

SPOUSE'S CONTRIBUTION TO THE ECONOMIC CONDITION
OF AUTHORS

The large gap between typical total personal and total family income of authors points to the contributions of working spouses. Roughly two-thirds of the authors were married; 80 percent of married authors had spouses in the labor force. And spouses in

Income

many cases contributed significantly to the economic condition of the author. However, overall figures of spouses' financial contributions masked important differences between husbands and wives. Even in terms of labor force participation there was a predictable difference: 86 percent of the husbands of married female authors had a paid occupation compared with 64 percent of the wives of married male authors.[26] Far more important, the extent of contributions to household income by spouses depended in great measure on the sex of the spouse. The median income of female authors' husbands ran to some $26,000, but the corresponding median income of male authors' wives was just $4,000. Moreover, a quarter of the husbands of female authors earned at least $40,000 in 1979, while wives of male authors who earned $15,000 were in the best paid quarter of this group.

These data suggest that married female authors were generally much more dependent on their spouses for material support than were married male authors. On the one hand, the wife of a male author typically accounted for a tenth of the total family income; the male author predominantly supported by a working wife was highly uncommon. On the other hand, the husband of a female author typically earned 62 percent of the family income; a quarter contributed more than 84 percent.[27] Thus we find that many husbands were in a position to "subsidize " their wives' writing, but few wives did so.[28]

Changes in Authors' Incomes

To assess whether there has been any change in the economic condition of American authors, we compared the incomes of present-day authors to those reported by writers in a study, *How Authors Make a Living*, conducted by William J. Lord, Jr. in 1957. Whatever the comparative figures, there are good reasons to treat the results as only provisional. For one thing, Lord's study was based on a survey of Authors League members, and his response rate of 18 percent raises even more concern about response bias than our less than desirable 46 percent. Second, the income categories used by our study are

TABLE 4.10. A Comparison of Authors' 1957 and 1978 Writing Incomes

Income Bracket	1957	1978
$ 0–$ 3,150	22%	37%
$ 3,151–$ 5,250	7	12
$ 5,251–$ 10,500	14	16
$ 10,501–$ 21,000	20	14
$ 21,001–$ 31,520	9	8
$ 31,521–$ 52,520	14	5
$ 52,521–$105,050	7	5
$105,051–$210,000	5	2
$210,001 +	2	1
	100%	100%
	(223)	(1,619)

Note: The values for 1957 come from Lord's study. Lord's percentages represent all writing income, including salaried income. The 1978 values do not represent salaried income; they include income directly related to writing and other freelance writing income (see text). The income brackets were inflated from 1957 dollars to 1978 dollars.

similar but not identical to the categories used by Lord. The figures for 1957 include "personal income earned by the writer from any salaried or commissioned writing assignment"; and our data include only income from the combined categories of "income directly related to [freelance] writing" (e.g., royalties from books, income from magazine articles, etc.) and "income from other freelance writing work." The salaried income of a journalist or an advertising copywriter, for example, would be included in Lord's data and not in ours. Despite these deficiencies in the data sets, the results lead to some intriguing suggestions.

Table 4.10 compares authors' incomes from writing in 1957 and in 1978.[29] The data indicate that, in general, authors made slightly less from writing in 1978 than they did in 1957. In 1957, about 37 percent of the authors made more than $21,000 annually from writing; in 1978, 21 percent did that well. More notably, in 1957, 22 percent of the authors made $3,150 or less annually; 37 percent of the authors in 1978 were in this category. These data suggest that the economic prospects facing the would-be full-time writer were absolutely no better than they were twenty-one years before. If any pattern is identifiable in these data, it

TABLE 4.11. A Comparison of Authors' 1957 and 1978 Total Family Incomes

Income Bracket	1957	1978
$ 0–$ 3,150	18%	2%
$ 3,151–$ 5,250	6	2
$ 5,251–$ 10,500	14	6
$ 10,501–$ 21,000	22	15
$ 21,001–$ 31,520	12	19
$ 31,521–$ 52,520	16	29
$ 52,521–$105,050	7	20
$105,051–$210,000	4	6
$210,001 +	1	2
	100%	101%
	(438)	(1,622)

Note: The values for 1957 come from Lord's study. The income brackets were inflated from 1957 dollars to 1978 dollars (see text).

is that the probability of living poorly from full-time writing has increased.[30]

Consider now the total family income of authors in 1957 and in 1978 (see table 4.11). Our category "total family income" refers to the same earnings included in Lord's category "all writers total income from all sources." This measure includes an author's income from writing and non-writing activities and the income of his/her spouse. According to these data, authors were more comfortable in 1978 than they were two decades before. In 1957 more than one-third of the authors surveyed had annual family incomes of $10,500 (1978 dollars) or less. Only 10 percent of our respondents reported family incomes that low for 1978. Three quarters of our respondents reported annual family incomes for 1978 that were greater than $21,000; in 1957 only 40 percent of the authors had family incomes that high.

The pattern of lower incomes from writing but higher family incomes is difficult to explain. We might speculate that the decline in economic return to writing may have prompted authors to give greater efforts to relatively well paid nonwriting endeavors, thus increasing their total incomes. However, we have no direct evidence of any such change in occupational commitment, and these decades were a time of a substantial, general increase in real family income.

A Concluding Perspective

The analysis of income and the prior discussion of occupational commitments of authors can hardly reinforce any imagery of glamour surrounding the writing of a book. By focusing on the economic condition of authors, however, we have purposefully underscored the fact that even for authors there is a cash nexus and a mundane side of the job, like other jobs, in which one is simply trying to make a living. These aspects of the profession of author are to be acknowledged, just as is the importance of the enterprise in defining and constructing culture. To some, a concern with the economic standing of authors may seem to taint the significance of their important contributions to cultural enrichment and change. But for the men and women who write, these economics are constraining and inescapable.

And yet, quite plainly, authors are an interesting lot because of their central role in the creation of our culture. We turn in the next chapter to the social and professional contexts in which authors make this distinctive contribution.

5.

Social and Professional Connections Among Authors

> If I had to give young writers advice,
> I would say don't listen to writers
> talk about writing or themselves.
> Lillian Hellman

THE ACT OF freelance writing is, of course, almost inevitably a solitary pursuit, only occasionally performed, outside of academic disciplines, with a collaborator or two. The isolation imposed by the task perhaps prompted Hemingway to remark that "writing is the loneliest trade."[1] While the practice of the trade may be carried out alone, writers are not necessarily social isolates. We encounter stories, some undoubtedly apocryphal, of the comings and goings of certain prominent writers—drinking together at favorite hangouts, summering at particular resorts, meeting at promotional bashes or award ceremonies, coming together in workshops. These accounts anecdotally suggest that not only are authors sociable but they are sociable with others within the writers' ranks, or at least that some authors are.

However, we also are told by such astute observers of the writing scene as Bellow (1977), Cowley (1954), and Coser, Kadushin, and Powell (1982), almost as common wisdom, that American authors are a highly disconnected lot with little contact with each other. These commentators necessarily rely on their impressionistic sense of matters, not systematic evidence; but typically the point of comparison is some intense literary society—exemplified by the coffee houses and salons of London or Paris in past eras—presumed to characterize cultural life in certain European societies. Commenting on the American literary scene and his own experience, Bellow writes: "No tea at Gertrude Stein's, no Closerie de Lilas, no Bloomsbury evenings, no charming and wicked encounters between George Moore and W. B. Yeats.... I can't say I miss them, because I never knew anything like them" (1977:182).

Quite clearly, such prominent and densely linked networks of authors have existed in England and on the Continent among a literary elite, and perhaps did so in early twentieth-century America. These circles seem to have been conduits for the diffusion of ideas, while providing social support for the innovative endeavor and creating and defining broad patterns of cultural taste. If so, the character of a society's literature would seem to be in part conditioned by the social organization of its producers.

Yet we really do not know how extensive literary circles were or are now, nor to what extent nonelite authors were or are involved in them or tied to each other. The social organization of authors as a whole may have been and may still be quite different from that of the elite. Indeed, it would be surprising if this were not so, but the evidence necessary to assess this matter has not been available. Perhaps in previous eras it was sufficient to study these prominent circles in order to understand literary cultural life because the ranks of authors were comparatively so small. Now, however, with the modern book explosion and greater cultural variety, it is useful to examine the patterns of social exchange within a greater range of authors, among both the elite and the nonelite.

We describe here, with systematic but limited data, some general patterns of social connection among American authors. More particularly, we will suggest that authors have limited professional relationships and sociable ties with each other. In addition to characterizing the overall patterns within this disparate group, we will specify how these connections differ among broadly defined types. The aggregate responses to a handful of survey questions can hardly provide a refined view of the

Connections Among Authors

social organization among authors. A sense of nuance, individual distinctiveness, and subjective meaning is inevitably lacking; but these questions do allow for the first orderly mapping.

As indicated, we distinguish between professional and sociable connections. We look at professional, work-related connections as those arising from personal interactions which specifically focus on the authors' writing. By contrast, sociable connections entail social encounters, friendships, and the like not necessarily involving consideration of the authors' own writing. Certainly this distinction cannot be viewed as hard and fast, and yet it points to important different ways in which authors may be tied together. As much as possible, it seems worth distinguishing between the connection involved in, say, two authors who critique each others' writing and that between two authors who play tennis together and exchange light, offhand comments about popular taste in literature or "writer's block." By considering both of these types of connections, we can provide a more complete picture of the social organization of the occupation and the nature of the connections authors have with each other.

We recognize that the boundary between these two spheres may often be difficult to distinguish in the lives of many authors. The two may easily meld together—as, say, professors eating lunch at the faculty club, poets drinking together at a neighborhood bar, or mystery writers meeting at a convention. And authors are certainly not unique in this respect. Where business ends and social life begins is often not clearly drawn, especially for many executives and professionals—whether on the golf course, at a cocktail party, or at an office softball game. Indeed, these mixed social-professional encounters often critically affect work life.

For this reason, after considering first the authors' professional ties and then their sociable encounters, we analyze how the professional and social spheres are tied together.

Professional Relationships with Other Authors

To get some sense of how frequently authors turn to professional colleagues for assistance in their work, we first asked, "Do you seriously discuss ideas for books or work in progress with other authors?" The inclusion of the word "seriously" may increase the ambiguity of the question, but we hoped it would prompt the respondents to distinguish between offhand, often fleeting remarks with fellow writers and more intense conversation which materially affected their own writing. Whether by personal choice or because suitable colleagues were unavailable, it is striking that relatively few authors had serious discussions about their writing with their fellow writers. Less than a tenth (8%) claimed to discuss their books "always" with other authors; another 12 percent did so "usually." The much more common pattern was to engage the thoughts of fellow authors "sometimes" (47%) or even "never" (32%).

Not only did authors rarely discuss their writing with other authors, but only a small number of colleagues were brought into such conversations when they did. We asked, "With how many authors did you seriously discuss your most recent work?" The most common answer was "zero"; 27 percent of the authors worked in such professional isolation. Another 31 percent talked with one or two authors; 22 percent, with three to five; and the remaining 11 percent talked to six or more.[2]

Even among the relatively few authors who discussed their work with colleagues, the extent of collegial contact tended to be limited. Of the authors who always discussed their books with fellow writers, about a quarter (24%) turned to one or two others on their last work, and another third (33%) talked with three to five. Among those who usually discussed their writing with authors, three-fourths (74%) engaged five or fewer colleagues on their last work. Those authors who sometimes sought reactions from fellow writers were by far the largest group (47%). And of members of this group, almost a quarter (24%) did not talk to any other writer about their last book, and almost half (46%) talked with one or two. Of course, authors may be reluctant to talk about their current projects, but it appears that those few authors who talked with their fellows about their writing were generally also those who talked to more of them.

That most authors rarely engaged professional colleagues in discussions about their writing suggests that literary life in America is rather diffuse. But such a conclusion could be misleading, since these overall figures encompass both part- and full-timers, poets and novelists, proflific and fledgling authors, to cite just a few of our now familiar types. Are the various groups of authors all of a kind? Do they exhibit patterns of limited professional interaction? After all, some authors regularly talked about their writing with other writers and some talked with quite a few. Is this simply a random difference or is it patterned?

Briefly, we can say that various types of authors were not distinctly inclined or disinclined to "talk writing" with fellow authors, at least not to any great extent. However, by considering the extent of professional interaction within various types of authors and noting the differences which existed, we can draw a more revealing picture of the social organization of American literary production.

OCCUPATIONAL COMMITMENTS

First, let us consider authors who had diverse commitments to writing as an occupation, measured by the hours they devoted to the craft and whether it was their sole occupational pursuit. Although these diverse commitments were associated with differences in economic rewards, they did not appear to be matched by notably distinctive patterns of professional interaction.

Among all five types of authors considered in our classification, from the committed full-timers to the marginal part-timers, slightly less than half in each group claimed that they sometimes discussed their writing with fellow writers.[3] Indeed, while full-time authors were slightly more inclined than those writing part-time to never discuss their writing with colleagues, most notable is the simple fact that the level of commitment of authors to their trade was virtually unrelated to the frequency of their professional interaction with other authors. Moreover, occupational commitment to writing was only very weakly related to the number of fellow writers consulted. Full-time authors had slightly fewer professional contacts than part-timers; among all types, a large majority discussed their most recent work with two or fewer fellow authors.

The Academic Exception. One group of part-time writers stood out in its pattern of professional interaction: university and college professors, who represented about a third of all part-time authors.

Fifteen percent of authors who also worked as professors said they always discussed their writing with fellow writers whereas 18 percent usually did. Roughly a third, then, of the academics have some regular professional interaction, almost twice the rate of both all full-time and all other part-time authors (18%). Not only did academics have more frequent professional contacts, but they also talked with more fellow writers about their writing. A fifth talked with six or more other authors about their most recent work; more than half (53%) did so with at least three others. In contrast, not even 10 percent of the full-time writers had talked with as many as six fellow authors, and only 27 percent had conversed with at least three others. Nonacademic, part-time writers were no different from the full-timers in the number of professional contacts.

In fact, the pattern among academic authors was so distinctive that it almost totally accounts for the very slight differences in the level of professional interaction between part- and full-time authors. If the professor-authors are excluded from the analysis, occupational commitment to writing turns out to be unrelated to patterns of professional interaction.

This academic exception represents no puzzle. At the university, fellow authors have offices right down the hall, and in the course of their professional academic involvements, professors routinely come into contact with other academics who write books. And if their books are oriented to an academic audience, professor-authors are almost enjoined to be in contact with others in their field. Indeed, "invisible colleges" with multiple interconnected networks of scholars and scientists sharing similar substantive interests are one of the hallmarks of contemporary academic science and scholarly communities. In short, both the physical proximity of other authors and the norms of collegiality enhance the probability that authors located in such academic settings will have high rates of professional interaction.[4]

WRITING ACTIVITY

One might presume that prolific authors have relatively high visibility within the profession, but such visibility does not translate into more frequent or a greater number of professional contacts. In

Connections Among Authors

fact, the relatively prolific authors were very slightly inclined to have less frequent professional talk and to speak with fewer fellow writers. These relationships are extremely weak, and no causal inferences are warranted. Moreover, the fact of being currently visible with a recently published book had no impact on either the regularity or the extent of professional interaction.

WRITING SUCCESS

For an author, success may be judged in various lights, but whether the criteria involve the rewards of the marketplace or honorific recognition, it was largely unrelated to patterns of professional interaction. That award-winning writers, even those who have been honored with the most prestigious awards, did not have distinctive patterns of professional interaction, at least as measured by our crude indicators, seems particularly remarkable. Many of the awards are granted by committees of professional peers, and the attendant ceremonies and general enhanced recognition by fellow writers would seem to make professional interaction at least relatively available. However, the major award winners were no more or less inclined than those honored with minor awards or those not honored at all to engage fellow authors regularly in "writing talk," or to engage a greater number.[5]

When success is measured in terms of money, it also did not seem to foster any distinctive tendency for authors to seek out or shun the reactions of fellow writers to their writing. Up to the extraordinarily fortunate few (3.5%) who earned in excess of $100,000 from their writing, there was virtually no variation by income level in the regularity with which authors talked about their work with fellow writers.[6] These fortunate few were just barely more apt to avoid professional conversations than their less well-rewarded counterparts. We further found that those authors with a recent best-seller did not have distinctive patterns of professional interaction.[7]

GENRE

Of course, by defining all book writers as belonging to a single occupation, we are in effect considering together the producers of diverse kinds of work—serious novels, gothic romances, how-to's, nonfiction for general audiences, academic tomes, and tales for children. Yet the technical skills and the psychic commitments required for writing would seem to differ depending on the type of book. We might therefore expect that these varying requirements may induce certain types of authors to seek out professional contact with fellow authors.

As table 5.1 indicates, authors of books in certain genres were in fact somewhat more regularly involved in professional dialogues about their writing than others. Again, the academic exception is readily apparent. A third of all authors who wrote for an academic audience talked with fellow writers always or usually about their work. As already noted, such discussions are normatively expected in many academic fields.

The only other group which matched this level of regular professional contact was the small number who identified themselves as poets. (Because there were very few poets in our sample, however, any inferences about this group must be cautiously drawn.) Almost a third of them also had fairly regular contact, and a relatively small number never had any peer contact about their writing. This higher level of association may result from the second job that poets often hold as teachers in colleges and universities. Whether poets in America really are "a kind of extended family, scattered in space and characterized by both the closeness of interest and the violence of dispute which often mark familial life," as Wilson (1958:178) contends, is a matter which we cannot adequately address. But by comparison to nonacademic writers of prose, poets appeared to be somewhat more inclined to talk about their writing with fellow authors.

There were not, however, distinctive patterns of professional contact among the authors who primarily committed their writing energies to one or the other side of the great divide between fiction and nonfiction. The authors of adult nonfiction were slightly more likely to talk regularly with fellow writers than authors of fiction, especially authors of genre fiction. And yet these differences were so small that it is plainly unwarranted to speak of some characteristic pattern of professional contact among authors of fiction which sets them apart from their nonfiction counterparts.

We may further add that the division between works for

TABLE 5.1. How Frequently Authors Discuss Their Writing with Other Authors: A Comparison of Selected Genres

Frequency of discussions[a]	Adult nonfiction	Academic nonfiction	Genre General fiction	Genre fiction	Children's books	How-to books	Poetry
Always	10%	17%	8%	4%	5%	7%	11%
Usually	13	16	9	12	11	10	22
Sometimes	49	46	45	46	50	46	51
Never	28	20	38	38	34	37	16
Total (rounded)	100%	99%	100%	100%	100%	100%	100%
	(535)	(249)	(395)	(267)	(323)	(134)	(37)

[a]Responses to "Do you seriously discuss ideas for books or works in progress with other authors?"

adults and children also did not mark distinctive patterns of professional contact. Compared to all other authors, writers of children's books were very slightly less inclined to talk regularly with other authors about their writing; but this was a minor tendency, not a pronounced difference in orientation.

Indeed, in considering the regularity of professional contacts among authors in different genres, we are again more struck by similarities than differences. In every genre, authors were by a large margin most likely to indicate that they sometimes talked with fellow writers about their writing—about half in each group—and more authors in each genre were apt to say they never talked to fellow writers than that they always talked to them.

THE DEMOGRAPHICS OF AUTHOR NETWORKS

In part, the extent and regularity of professional conversation depends on the simple availability of fellow writers. Thus, we noted, authors almost inevitably run into each other in academe, and their professional conversations are understandably relatively frequent. But, plainly, most authors do not have such professional encounters so routinely within their immediate environment. Whatever their inclinations, authors living in rustic hideaways or even Small Town, U.S.A., would seem to have fewer chances to talk with fellow writers than those living in cosmopolitan areas, especially New York.

As we documented, writers are not randomly scattered across the country; about a third of our sample lived in the New York metropolitan area, and another quarter lived in other parts of the Northeast. To be sure, no one has ever considered New York some large literary salon drawing authors together in intense collegiality, but the concentration of writers is nonetheless remarkable and consistent with the widely noted attraction of city life to those with an artistic temperament. It does at least suggest some pull, some unusual attraction to writers.

Yet if authors find New York especially congenial, it is more for its cultural resources and perceived access to publishers than because of a widespread pattern of intense professional interaction. While fellow authors may generally be more available to New York–

based writers, the regularity of professional contact among them was virtually the same as that for their counterparts across the country. Furthermore, the New York–based writers were not any more inclined than others to engage more than a few colleagues in conversations about their writing. In short, the great concentration of authors in New York has not led to a distinctively intense professional interaction which encompasses the broad range of authors living there.

The only regionalism of any note whatsoever on this matter relates to Southern writers. (About a tenth of the authors in our sample made their home in the South.) Compared to writers in other regions, they talked somewhat less regularly with fellow writers about their writing and also to fewer of them.

A number of personal characteristics had no, or only a minor, relationship to patterns of professional interaction. First, we found no differences between men and women authors. About a quarter of writers between the ages of thirty and fifty "talked writing" regularly (that is, always or usually), a rate about double that among their older and younger counterparts; but even among this most professionally interactive age group, irregular and few contacts with fellow authors were the rule. And finally, while the extent of occupational inheritance was high (about a fifth of all authors had a parent or other close relative who wrote a book), those authors who were "born into the trade" did not exhibit any distinctive patterns of professional interaction.

Work Relationships with Nonauthors

Authors' general reluctance to talk writing did not extend just to their professional counterparts. Complementary to the question about conversations with other authors, we asked, "Besides your relatives, do you seriously discuss ideas for books or work with people who are not authors?" In general, the answer was not with any great regularity. A third answered "never" and another half, "sometimes." About a tenth (11%) did so "usually" and only 6 percent, "always." This pattern of response virtually matched that for the regularity of writing talk with fellow authors.

This tendency not to discuss one's own writing with occupational outsiders did not, in general, differ significantly among types of authors. To a very slight degree, the committed part-timers (that is, those with another job but who wrote at least twenty-five hours a week) were relatively inclined to discuss their writing with others, but the regularity of these exchanges did not vary by type of other job for the part-timers, recency of publication, or writing success—financial or honorific.

As with the regularity of conversations about writing with fellow authors, however, there was some variation by genre. Yet again it was not a matter of particularly distinctive work styles. To illustrate this point, consider the authors with the greatest and the least tendency to discuss their writing with others—writers of adult nonfiction and children's books, respectively. Overall, 17 percent of the authors talked writing with occupational outsiders somewhat regularly; 24 percent of the authors of adult nonfiction and 10 percent of the authors of children's books did so.

Turning to the effects of where authors live, we again found a small amount of Southern distinctiveness. As with their slight tendency to have less professional contact, Southern authors were also somewhat less inclined to talk writing with outsiders. Twelve percent of them did so somewhat regularly as compared to the general rate of 17 percent; 43 percent of the Southerners never had these conversations, while a third of all authors never did. With such minor differences, however, one should certainly not infer that Southern writers personify some distinctive cultural pattern of an isolated work style. Nor are New York writers especially "involved": they were no more or less likely to discuss writing with nonauthors than were their counterparts across the country.

Whether avoidance of conversations about one's own writing with nonauthors represents the wisdom gained by age is an open issue, but older writers were notably less inclined than younger writers to talk about their work with others. Thirty-eight percent of the youngest writers (under thirty) and 27 percent of those thirty to thirty-nine had somewhat regular conversations with others; in contrast, the rate for those forty to forty-nine was 17 percent; for those fifty to sixty-four, 13 percent; and for the oldest writers, 7 percent.

Another open issue is whether there is any significance in the fact that male authors somewhat more regularly discussed their writing with others than female authors. Although there was no difference between the sexes in their tendency to talk writing with fellow writers, 19 percent of the men versus 13 percent of the women discussed their writing somewhat regularly with nonauthors, while 29 percent of men and 39 percent of the women never did.

Writing: Individualistic Work

Do most authors, then, construct their works without extensive professional conversations with their friends or professional associates? Are most of them "loners" while a few are "interactors"? Or do authors turn to one group or the other for consultation? That is, do authors who converse irregularly with fellow writers have regular professional discussions about their writing with others and vice versa?

In fact, we found no compensatory pattern: just the opposite was the case. As the top percentages in the cells of table 5.2 indicate, authors who were relatively inclined to discuss their writing with fellow writers also tended to discuss it with others. Thus about a quarter of the authors who always talked with fellow authors also always talked with others—a rate far higher than all others. And, relatedly, the authors who never spoke with fellow authors were most likely to never talk with nonauthors (52%) as well. But recognize that this is a matter of tendency. Whatever their inclination to talk writing with their professional peers, most authors did not regularly discuss their writing with others.

Indeed, we see that most authors did not regularly talk with professional peers *or* others (see table 5.2, percentages in parentheses). In response to the two questions about serious discussions of their writing, 17 percent never engaged colleagues or nonauthors, while 70 percent answered some combination of sometimes or never to both. By contrast,

TABLE 5.2. Relationship Between How Frequently Authors Discuss Their Writing with Other Authors and with Nonauthors

Frequency of Discussions with Authors[a]

Frequency of Discussions with Nonauthors[b]	Always	Usually	Sometimes	Never	Total
Always	24% (2%)	8% (1%)	4% (2%)	3% (1%)	6%
Usually	11% (1%)	25% (3%)	10% (5%)	6% (2%)	11%
Sometimes	44% (4%)	50% (6%)	59% (28%)	39% (13%)	50%
Never	21% (2%)	17% (2%)	26% (12%)	52% (17%)	33%
Total	100% (181)	100% (260)	99% (1002)	100% (692)	100% (2135)

Note: The top percentage within each cell is the column percentage; the percentages within the parentheses are the percentages of the total (2135).
[a] Responses to "Do you seriously discuss ideas for books or work in progress with other authors?"
[b] Responses to "Besides your relatives, do you seriously discuss ideas for books or work in progress with people who are not authors?"

the numbers indicating some regular serious discussions with both authors *and* others are very small: only 7 percent answered some combination of always or usually to the two questions. For the most part, then, authors work on their writing with little direct reaction from others. Authorship is commonly, at least in this sense, an individualistic act carried out with only irregular contributions from others, a finding which bears out Hemingway's assertion about a "lonely trade."

In detailing authors' general irregularity of writing talk with fellow authors and occupational outsiders, we do not mean to imply that this is some bad, undesirable state of affairs. In our interviews and in written responses on their questionnaires, many authors adamantly rejected the value of talking about their writing with others. One novelist claimed that fellow writers were almost inevitably petty, jealous, or dishonest. Another recounted how she and some other female writers had gotten together as a "support group" on a fairly regular basis to discuss their work; but after some time, she became disillusioned and stopped going because "I began to talk more about writing than actually write. I don't think I really got any help out of it."

Those having positive things to say generally cast their remarks in predictable ways. Other authors were seen as valuable "sounding boards" and sources of encouragement, technical advice, and "constructive" criticism. One wrote, "I talk with other authors because they know what I'm going through." Another told us that "authors are the best editors."

With the data at hand, we cannot accurately assess to what extent the frequency of discussions about writing is a matter of choice or necessity. However, only a few authors indicated a desire for more intense interaction with their fellow authors or others. Indeed, one of the reasons prompting people to choose writing as an occupation may be their desire to work in a relatively isolated way.

Sociable Contacts with Peers

Patterns of social engagement among authors gave further evidence of the structural diffuseness of the occupation. Most authors did not talk regularly about their writing with fellow authors, nor did they see them frequently on a social basis.

We asked the authors in our survey, "How often do you meet with other authors in some social setting? (Exclude your spouse.)" By far the most common response was "rarely"; just less than half (47%) answered this way. Almost another quarter (23%) responded "every few months." Much less common (19%) were those authors who socialized with fellow authors "at least once a month," and still fewer (10%) were those who did so "at least once a week."

Nor does a shared occupational commitment foster a wide network of friendships for most authors. To the question "How many other authors (excluding your spouse) do you count as a good friend?" the most common answer (19%) was zero. And those with many other author friends were relatively few: 27 percent had one or two friends; 30 percent had three to five; 14 percent had six to ten; and 10 percent had eleven or more.

As with patterns of professional interaction, there was little variation in the frequency and extent of sociable contacts across broad types of authors. To be sure, some minor differences appeared; but for all the diversity within the occupation, again the striking fact is the similarly low level of social contact which prevailed among groups of authors with such different circumstances and occupational and aesthetic commitments. For instance, once the unusually sociable group of author-professors was excluded, the part-time and full-time authors were remarkably similar in their frequency of encounters with fellow writers. Thirty percent of each group met socially with other authors at least once a month as opposed to 42 percent of the author-professors.

We also found that authors with widely different levels of financial success had largely similar patterns of social interaction. To a very slight degree, the large group who made virtually nothing (0-$2,500) from writing appeared the least sociable, but increased social contact with fellow authors did not go hand in hand with financial success. Only the relatively few earning $50,000-$99,999 were relatively sociable: 46 percent met with fellow writers at least once a month, and 31 percent had at least six author friends. (To appreciate the size of this "sociable" deviation, recall that for the sample as a whole 29 percent met socially with fellow authors at least once a month, while 24 percent had six or more author friends.) All the rest, including those who earned in excess of $100,000 and those with a recent best-seller, did not deviate appreciably from the general pattern in either frequency of contact or number of author friends.

While the financial rewards of writing were not consistently related to sociability among authors, there was some small tendency for the more honored writers to be more socially connected to their colleagues. Yet once again we are speaking of a matter of slight degree, not a distinctive pattern (see Table 5.3). Thus, 41 percent of those honored with a major award saw fellow authors socially at least once a month; 34 percent of those honored with a minor award and 27 percent of the nonhonored had such frequent social meetings. At the other extreme, a large contingent within each of these groups "rarely" socialized with fellow authors, but the likelihood varied: major award winners—37 percent; minor award winners—41 percent; and the nonhonored—52 percent.[8]

A similarly modest relationship also held between honorific recognition and the number of author friends.[9] That is, honored writers tended to have a few more such friends than the others; but even so, critical recognition did not bring with it a large number of friends from the writers' ranks. Just less than a third of those honored with a major award counted at least six fellow authors as good friends (compared to 24 percent of the total sample).

Across all the large genres, the most prevalent pattern was to meet with fellow authors rarely. Only the authors of how-to and children's books had low levels of somewhat regular contact, and these differences were very slight. Furthermore, no genre seemed to foster a particularly large number of author friends, and only the how-to writers had a relatively restricted set of friends from the ranks of authors. (Sixty-two percent of them had two or fewer author friends; for the total sample the proportion was 46 percent.)

Although what authors wrote had only a very small effect on their patterns of socializing, where they wrote did make some difference. The "New York factor" deserves particular attention. With the great concentration of authors in the New York area, one might expect particularly intense interaction, of both a professional and a social nature. Recall, though, that we found nothing distinctive about

TABLE 5.3. How Often Authors Meet Socially with Other Authors: Differences by Honorific Recognition

	Honor[a]			
Frequency of social meetings[b]	No award	Minor award	Major award	Total
Once a week	10%	11%	14%	11%
Once a month	17	23	27	20
Every few months	22	25	22	23
Rarely	52	41	37	46
Total (rounded)	101%	100%	100%	100%
	(1028)	(695)	(181)	(1904)

[a]Appendix D presents the classification of major and minor awards.
[b]Responses to "How often do you meet with other authors in some social setting?"

Connections Among Authors

their professional interaction. Nonetheless, the New York–based authors were more likely than others to meet socially on a somewhat regular basis with fellow writers. Thirty-seven percent of the New Yorkers got together with fellow writers at least once a month, 16 percent at least once a week. The respective figures for all the non–New Yorkers were 28 percent and 8 percent. Even so, the greatest number of New York (40%) and non–New York writers (50%) rarely met socially with fellow authors. In line with their greater professional isolation, the Southern writers were also the least apt to meet socially in a regular way, though this was only a slight tendency.

Indeed, the significance of the New York factor should not be overdrawn. Even if they did meet a little more frequently with fellow authors, their circles of author friends were generally no broader than those of their counterparts across the country. Like the rest, almost half of the New Yorkers had no more than two good friends among the ranks of authors. Moreover, Southerners, appearing relatively isolated in other ways, did not differ appreciably from the general pattern. All this detail adds up to a decided lack of regionalism in the extent to which authors were connected to other authors through friendship.

In sum, there were generally no distinctive patterns of sociable interaction across broad groups of authors in terms of time commitment to writing, financial success from it, or a number of personal characteristics, including age, sex, and a writing family background. The only notable exceptions to this conclusion involved the most honored members of the occupation and those living in New York, the area of greatest concentration. The award winners were slightly inclined to be more frequently and extensively connected to fellow writers, but intense interaction was by no means common even for them. New York–based writers met more frequently with other authors (although they did not have more author friends), but infrequent contact was still their rule. Yet even with a few small exceptions, the overall lack of patterning in social engagement, like that for professional interaction, was the most remarkable point.

The Social-Professional Connection

In what we have designated the social and professional realms, then, authors appear to be a loosely connected lot, and yet as we indicated at the beginning of this chapter, these realms may not be entirely separate parts of their lives. Indeed, for many authors they may be vitally and subtly linked. A few survey items plainly do not allow detailed analysis of this matter. However, by examining the relationships between what we called the authors' sociable and professional ties, a more complete picture of how the occupation is socially organized may emerge. Thus we consider the following: the relationship between social and professional interaction (are the more socially engaged also more professionally connected?); and the distribution of authors by the extent of social and professional encounters (what proportions are loosely connected on both counts, intensely involved on both counts, etc.?)

In the aggregate, a connection between the social and professional realms was notable: the more frequent the social encounters, the more regular discussions about writing with fellow authors (see table 5.4). To see the strength of this connection, consider first the regularity of writing-related discussions among the authors who socially see other authors at least once a week. Among this small sociable minority, more than half (57%) at least somewhat regularly discussed their writing with fellow authors and only a tenth avoided these conversations. At the other extreme, the social isolates of the profession—that is, the great number who rarely socialized with fellow authors—only infrequently turned to other writers for professional opinions. Six percent did so somewhat regularly, about half never did. And between these extremes of sociability, those with more frequent social contact were apt to have more regular professional discussions, even if conversations of this sort were generally not the rule.

In detailing the general relationship between social and professional encounters, we do not want to obscure the critical point: the infrequent contact of authors with each other in both ways measured in this study. The largest proportion, 24 percent, never discussed their writing with fellow authors *and* rarely socialized with them. An-

TABLE 5.4. Relationship Between the Frequency of Social and Professional Contacts Among Authors

Frequency of Social Meetings[a]

Frequency of writing discussions[b]	Once a week	Once a month	Every few months	Rarely	Total
Always	28% (3%)	16% (3%)	6% (1%)	2% (1%)	8%
Usually	29% (3%)	21% (4%)	15% (3%)	4% (2%)	12%
Sometimes	33% (4%)	51% (10%)	60% (14%)	43% (20%)	47%
Never	11% (1%)	13% (2%)	20% (5%)	51% (24%)	32%
Total (rounded)	101% (233)	101% (417)	101% (485)	100% (1003)	99% (2138)

Note: The top percentage within each cell is the column percentage; the percentages within the parentheses are the percentages of the total (2138).
[a]Responses to "How often do you meet with other authors in a social setting?"
[b]Responses to "Do you seriously discuss ideas for books or works in progress with other authors?"

other fifth talked about writing sometimes and socialize rarely with other authors. Correlatively, only a small minority of authors, some 13 percent, discussed their writing at least usually and socialized at least once a month with other writers. And just a few percent had what may be considered intense social and professional engagement—that is, always discussing their writing and socializing at least once a week.

In further considering the connection between the social and professional realms of the occupation, we also found that authors with a greater number of author friends were also relatively inclined to talk writing more regularly with fellow writers (see table 5.5). Thus, more than a third of the authors with six or more author friends always or usually discussed their writing with their colleagues. In contrast, less than a sixth of the authors with one or two author friends had such regular professional contact, and virtually none of those without an author friend did. In other words, without friendships with authors, professional contact was rare.

We found as well that the greater the number of author friends, the greater the number of authors involved in professional discussions related to a writer's most recent work. By no means did authors with many author friends necessarily engage many peers in talk about their own writing (see table 5.6). For instance, of the writers with six or more author friends, about a fifth talked with only one or two fellow writers about their last work, and another fifth talked with no fellow writer. But, still, there was a notable tendency for authors with relatively wide social connections with other writers to also have relatively extensive professional connections, even the two together were generally uncommon.

Together, these findings consistently suggest a link between an author's professional and social connections with fellow writers. To a notable extent, those authors who were more socially active with other authors were also more involved with them about their writing.

There are important limits to these data, however. First, we cannot say whether authors with frequent and extensive social contacts with other authors turned to these same authors for professional opinions about their writing. It certainly seems likely that authors would tend to feel most comfortable discussing their writing

TABLE 5.5. Relationship Between the Number of Author Friends and Frequency of Writing-related Discussions

Frequency of Discussions[a]	Number of Author Friends				
	0	1–2	3–5	6+	Total
Always	2%	4%	10%	18%	9%
Usually	2	9	16	19	12
Sometimes	25	57	54	46	47
Never	71	30	21	17	32
Total (rounded)	100%	100%	101%	100%	100%
	(398)	(561)	(618)	(484)	(2061)

[a]Responses to "Do you seriously discuss ideas for books or work in progress with other authors?"

TABLE 5.6. Relationship Between the Number of Authors Involved in Discussions of Most Recent Work and the Number of Author Friends

	Number of Author Friends				
Number of Authors in Writing Discussions	0	1–2	3–5	6+	Total
0	77% (14%)	35% (10%)	25% (8%)	21% (5%)	36%
1–2	13% (2%)	51% (14%)	32% (10%)	21% (5%)	31%
3–5	7% (1%)	12% (3%)	34% (10%)	29% (7%)	22%
6+	3% (1%)	3% (1%)	9% (3%)	29% (7%)	11%
Total (rounded)	100% (321)	101% (496)	100% (550)	100% (415)	100% (1782)

Note: The top percentage within each cell is the column percentage; the percentages within the parentheses are the percentages of the total (1782).

Connections Among Authors

with good friends—after all, it is a favor—but friends may also be unapproachable because of their personal closeness, the special difficulties of giving and receiving criticism, the jealousies which may be difficult to manage. Whatever the case, our data do not directly show how an individual author's professional and social networks among authors are connected.

Second, the analysis only establishes correlations, not causal relationships. We have considered how social contacts are related to professional contacts, but we cannot say, on the basis of these data, that intense social interaction causes intense professional interaction (or vice versa). Sociable meetings and friendships could be a basis for later professional talk, but at the same time conversations about writing among professional acquaintances may lead to friendship and involvement in wider social networks. Indeed, it may be best to see professional and social connections as reinforcing each other, producing some loose structure within this otherwise diffuse occupation.

A third limitation lies in our focus on the connections individual authors had with fellow authors, rather than on the social organization of the occupation per se. While we have shown that most authors had infrequent and limited contacts with their professional counterparts, we cannot say anything about the structure of the personal *networks* within the occupation. To delineate this network structure, it is necessary to know who socialized and had professional contacts with whom. We lack such relational data. By pointing to the large number of social and professional isolates, however, our individual-level data certainly suggest that dense networks are likely to be quite uncommon.

Patterns of Influence

Writing, like other forms of artistic production, is inevitably in part a social process. However individualistic the act of writing, no one writes in a social vacuum. At minimum, general frames of reference which structure meaning, modes of expression, and stylistic conventions are affected by prevailing cultural patterns. Additionally, and more directly, some authors may be influenced by peers on specific matters of style, theme, and the like. Undoubtedly, this process is varied, subtle, conditioned by individual personality, and furthered in a host of ways.

Personal contact is obviously one way in which social influences are transmitted. While we do not analyze most of the complexities of this process, our finding on the low level of professional and social connections among authors does at least indirectly suggest that personal ties play a small role. Moreover, by their own accounts, authors themselves do not see private relationships with fellow writers as greatly influencing their work.

To see the authors' own views on the importance of personal ties, we asked, "Of the three contemporary authors who have most significantly influenced your own writing, what is the closest relationship you have?" The question is intended to tap the extent to which some important influences on authors' intellectual creation are personally transmitted. Plainly, the question contains some inherent ambiguities (among them that not all authors can readily specify three such influential contemporaries); but it does provide a rough indication of whether authors have personal connections to a contemporary whom they view as at least relatively influential for their own writing.

In indicating the closest relationship they had among their influential contemporaries, the authors responded as follows:

- none has significantly influenced my work, 33 percent;
- "know" him or her only through published writing, 33 percent;
- have had some conversations, 6 percent;
- friendly acquaintanceship, 9 percent;
- friend, 15 percent;
- other, 4 percent.

The overwhelming majority of authors simply did not have a close personal link to writers who have had an important effect on their own work; only a quarter had any friendly relationships at all.

The perceived lack of any influence of contemporaries for

Connections Among Authors

so many is both remarkable and difficult to interpret. As outside observers, we find it difficult to believe that every author has not at least to some extent indirectly absorbed general frames of reference—not necessarily accepting the most conventional—through reading the writings of contemporaries. And even if an author considers the works of past eras to be more inspiring, contemporary writing would almost inevitably seem a source for stylistic and thematic borrowings or counterpoints for creative departures. Perhaps it is the very diffuseness of influences from contemporaries which led so many authors to claim that none exist, or, at least, not to recognize them among the somewhat artificial set "of the three contemporary authors who most influenced your own writing." We might also speculate that the usually solitary involvement in the actual act of writing a book may often foster a heightened sense of individualistic endeavor, a feeling of going it alone. Authors may even consider it normatively appropriate not to acknowledge influence, a way to affirm their own originality and achievement. Whatever the case, the fact that a third acknowledged no significant influence from a contemporary and another third had only an impersonal, intellectual connection points to the social organization of the occupation as an unimportant part of the literary production process. Certainly the influences of author friends were not sufficiently direct and consequential to be consciously recognized by many authors.

This conclusion generally held across the board for the groups of authors considered in previous sections of this chapter—the different occupational types, those with various levels of financial and critical success, the prolific and the little published, men and women, those from writing families and those not, and writers from various regions. Moreover, the likelihood of a personal relationship did not progressively increase with the job experience loosely suggested by age; while a slight tendency occurred for younger writers (under thirty) to know influential contemporaries only through their work, the oldest writers (sixty-five and older) were most likely to cite both no influence (45%) and a friend (18%). Once again, we can point to the academic exception, though it is not all that exceptional. Thirty-two percent counted a friend or friendly acquaintance as a significant influence; the overall rate was 24 percent. But still, 27 percent of the academics cited no contemporary as a significant influence, not much less than the total proportion.[10]

It is notable, however, that in certain genres authors were relatively likely to have personal connection with an influential contemporary. However, as table 5.7 indicates, the differences were not greatly marked. Adult nonfiction writers were slightly more inclined than their fiction-writing counterparts to have a friendly connection: 26 percent of the former included a friend or friendly acquaintance as a significant influence, in contrast to 20 percent of the latter. At the same time, virtually equal proportions of the fiction and nonfiction authors saw no contemporary as a significant influence on their writing.

The writers of academically oriented nonfiction and the very few poets stood out as the most likely to have personal connections to fellow writers who have influenced their own work. That almost a third of the poets had a friend who has had an important influence, more than double the overall rate, was especially remarkable.[11] Indeed, the poets represented the only genre in which a majority of the writers claimed at least some personal connection to an influential contemporary, a fact further supporting Wilson's (1958) sense of poets as an "extended family." At the other extreme, the writers of children's and how-to books claimed virtually no influence.

Literary Life and the Sociology of Culture

Whether these findings on the connections among authors do more to upset or confirm prevailing views we cannot say, simply because images of authors as both a cliquish lot and isolated loners seem current. But they do clearly and consistently lead us to conclude that the overwhelming number of authors have very limited or no personal connections to their writing counterparts, either of a professional, writing-related nature, or on a social level. Most authors do not talk about their writing with fellow writers (or anyone else), meet socially

TABLE 57. The Personal Influence of Contemporary Authors: A Comparison of Selected Genres

Kind of Relationship[a]	Adult nonfiction	Academic nonfiction	General fiction	Genre fiction	Children's books	How-to books	Poetry
None have significant influence	31	27	30	28	43	47	28
"Know" only through writing	34	23	43	44	30	28	19
Some conversations	6	9	5	4	5	4	8
Friendly acquaintanceship	12	11	9	7	7	6	11
Friend	14	24	11	13	12	12	31
Other	3	5	3	5	4	2	3
TOTAL (rounded)	100% (507)	99% (230)	101% (382)	101% (257)	101% (306)	99% (125)	100% (36)

[a]Responses to "Of the three contemporary authors who have most significantly influenced your own writing, what is the closest relationship you have?"

with them on a frequent basis, count many as good friends, or personally know any who have importantly influenced their own writing. Moreover, this disconnectedness cuts across a large number of author types and groups.

No doubt, the aggregated responses to a handful of survey questions provide a limited base for assaying the social organization among authors. Especially with prestructured answers we lose a sense of nuance; and in the statistical aggregation (even though various "types" are considered), we inevitably neglect the individual circumstance or the possibly distinctive inclinations of some small groups. But for the first time it is possible to go beyond the anecdotal to specify what is the typical pattern for authors in general and for broadly defined groups of authors.

In relating just what is typical (and deviant), we are limited to a few crude indicators of connections—the number of author friends, frequency of social encounters, etc. Of course, these only circumscribe broad aspects of the interactions among authors, but we consider them fundamental. While one may well wonder about the subjective meaning of the writing talk authors have with their fellows, it is critical to recognize that such conversations could not have much meaning for many simply because they are so infrequent. Similarly, one may want to know what authors do together in social settings and what consequences these meetings have, but it is again critical to know how uncommmon these encounters are. In the most basic ways, then, these indicators all point to the general social disconnectedness of the occupation, a condition which necessarily affects other aspects of interaction among authors.

Throughout this chapter, we have referred to the general disconnectedness of authors, their "thinness" of interaction, the limited extent of their ties, and a diffuse social organization. But one might well ask, as compared to what? What standards have we implicitly used?

No set of standards exists for such evaluative judgments, nor is it possible to advance any systematic standards of compelling validity. We certainly cannot turn to comparable surveys of people in other occupations for useful comparisons. Some loose points of reference, however, did shape these judgments.

Connections Among Authors

We were inevitably drawn to consider the common image of literary life in some European capitals. By comparison to that image of intense interaction, the connections among American authors as a whole appear low. The very prevalence of this image makes it an obvious point of reference, but the limits of the comparison must be underscored. Accounts of intimate personal connections among authors in European cities are largely impressionistic; systematic, quantitative data detailing the nature and extent of these connections are lacking. Also, these impressions seem based on the experience of literary elites, and it is impossible to say with any precision how encompassing these circles are or to what extent those outside the prominent circles are connected to each other. We certainly cannot say with any confidence whether the general pattern of interactions among, say, British or French authors is notably different from that among American authors.

Nevertheless, we can draw a somewhat sharper, though still very provisional, contrast by focusing on the patterns among our own literary elite and the residents of our "cultural capital." Recall that the relationships among the most honored American writers (i.e., those designated as major award winners) did not stand out as distinctly more intense than those among the nonelite. The major award winners were only slightly more socially connected and no more professionally linked than all others. It is reasonable to suggest therefore that the American elite's "connectedness" is low by comparison to their European counterparts. Moreover, those who live in the New York area—still our cultural capital, even if its dominance is less complete than in earlier eras—do not generally show any of the "incestuousness" which figures in the descriptions of literary life in European capitals. Although a greatly disproportionate number of American and European authors live in their cultural capitals, this proximity has not given rise to any all-encompassing literary life in New York. Again, we lack solid evidence, but in relation to the common impressionistic sense of what literary life is like in European capitals, the links among New York writers seem loose.

As another point of comparison, the disconnectedness among authors sharply contrasts with the density of connectedness among producers of a different form of culturally significant work, namely, academically based scientists. They make the lion's share of fundamental new discoveries, and even if they represent an elite, their patterns of interaction may be compared with the author elites or with academically based authors.

Not only is formal collaboration with a number of colleagues on projects common (see, for example, Hagstrom 1976), but elite scientists are usually linked to their professional colleagues in "invisible colleges," informal networks of researchers at different institutions working on similar problems (Price 1963; Crane 1972). Studies of various disciplines and subspecialties indicate that these networks differ in size, internal coherence, and patterns of interaction (Burt 1982). But even if the ties within these networks are often weak, the vastly greater interaction among scientists than authors is plainly highlighted by a recent estimate that fifty "individual professional workers" are typically linked in these networks (Hagstrom 1976). This estimate is subject to debate, depending as it does on the definition of a link, but the relatively greater professional connectedness among scientists is not in doubt. And, relatedly, the social organization of the scientific enterprise—entailing socialization at both personal and intellectual levels and controls over what is produced—is relatively structured as well.

With this relatively structured organization, it is extremely unlikely that any scientist would claim that no colleague had a significant influence on his or her work or that those with influence were known only through their writing. Academic chemists, for example, in Hagstrom's study (1976) reported spending, on average, more than four hours a week on professional correspondence, and some three-fifths of them spent at least six days a year at professional meetings.

While these differences in the overall pattern of connections among the producers in these two cultural realms are dramatic, the extent of interaction within each realm also differs. Sociologists of science (e.g., Merton 1973; Zuckerman 1978; Sullivan, White, and Barboni; Cole 1978; Cole and Cole 1973; Price 1963) have repeatedly shown that those scientists making the greatest intellectual contributions tend to be the most intensely involved in professional networks. In effect, they serve as the deans of the invisible colleges, directing the activities of their colleagues within their own work group and dealing with those in other networks. Thus intellectual prominence and social integration into the scientific community generally go hand in hand.

To draw the contrast again, the honored authors—those we may loosely consider as making the greatest contribution in the literary realm—are not in any distinctive way connected to fellow authors. This is not to deny that certain critically esteemed writers have intense ties to colleagues, nor to deny that within small sets of writers (poets, perhaps) the more esteemed may be somewhat more connected. Some intense occupational communities may exist among smaller "super elite" groups which our measures of recognition and linkage do not detect. But the critical elite, as we somewhat crudely and inclusively define them here, do not generally assume a prominent socially integrating role. Moreover, if the marketplace may be deemed the arbiter of literary contribution or elite status, the most financially successful authors do not take on this role either. Thus, while the reward structure of science systematically gives a prominent role to the elite within the personal networks of the scientific community, such is not the case within the more disparate literary community.

To a far lesser extent, the connections among artists, producers of culturally significant work in still another realm, were also an implicit point of reference. A few accounts suggest that intense interactions developed among fairly large sets of painters at particular times—e.g., among the Impressionists in France (White and White 1965) and the abstract expressionists in New York (Rosenberg and Fliegel 1965). Contemporary American literary life seems to lack analogous connectedness, even among critical and financial elites. However, the very notability of these ties among painters may suggest their distinctiveness. To what extent painters (and other artists) not involved in such relatively rare aesthetic revolutions are linked to each other is not systematically known.

Although the evidence is thin, that there are diversities in the connectedness among the producers of culture in different realms or societies is neither a surprising nor a remarkable claim. Yet it is a measure of the underdeveloped state of the sociology of culture that we are not able to specify these differences (and similarities) with any precision. If we are to understand sociologically how culture is actually produced, the collection of comparable information on the connections among the producers should be a central concern.[12] But while we sorely lack the necessary data for detailed comparisons across cultural domains or societies, we suggest that the gross differences in the connectedness among such "culture producers" as scientists and authors are at least theoretically expectable in a sociological perspective.

Charles Kadushin's (1976) suggestion of applying the concept "external economy" to culture production is useful for this purpose. Borrowed from the literature on industrial organization, this concept points to the necessary production-related factors that are available only outside the production unit. Factories, law firms, hospitals, scientific research teams, and solitary authors may all be considered production units. These factors could include supplies of various sorts (raw materials, ancillary manpower, innovative ideas) from other industries as well as other producers within the industry. Industries with a high dependence on external factors are considered an "external economy industry"; the women's high-fashion industry, the investment industry, and advertising are obvious examples. To illustrate, high-fashion garment makers all depend on designers, specialty suppliers, subcontractors with specialized skills, and each other—a source from which to steal ideas. In a similar way, "industries" involved in the production of culture—film, theater, art, and science, to cite prominent examples—are heavily dependent on external factors, though the nature of their external economies differ.

Generally, we propose, the more the external economy of a cultural area technically and materially depends on the actions of fellow producers, the greater the personal connectedness among the producers in that realm. While not discounting possible psychologically rooted differences in the sociable or collaborative dispositions of, say, biologists and novelists, this perspective emphasizes the role of social structural factors in fostering personal connections. Thus, variations in the external economies of writing and science, as examples of two cultural industries, account, at least in part, for differences in the interaction among producers.

To see how the difference between authors and scientists may be structurally induced, recognize first that scientists in many

Connections Among Authors

fields and specialties depend on the contributions of others in their field for the production of ideas, not just for the added benefits of intellectual stimulation or social support. Not only may collaboration be required to carry out some specific project, but scientists must be aware of the activities of other teams, so they can know that their own research will represent an original contribution and so they can acquire prepublication information which will help them make this contribution. Collaboration is the norm in most experimental sciences, and in the world of Big Science (Price 1963) it has become a necessity. This is not so in writing.

Today we can see the extreme interdependency of scientists in some areas of experimental physics. Eighty to a 100 scientists may collaborate on a single set of experiments, and while not common, the listing of authors in some journal articles requires more space than the content of the article itself. Indeed, the size of author sets in science has gotten so large in some specialty areas that not all the authors of the same paper know each other. At the other extreme, some theoretical physicists and mathematicians require only a pad and pencil and little external support or connectedness. While they depend on the extant literature, they do not depend on other scientists as a lifeline of ideas required for their own scientific production.

For the most part, especially among writers of fiction, the dependence of authors on their colleagues for the creation of ideas is minor. Books can be readily produced by an individual or a few collaborators; indeed, it is difficult even to imagine "writing teams" in many genres. Agatha Christie once said: "I've always believed in writing without a collaborator, because where two people are writing the same book, each believes he gets all the worries and only half the royalties." In addition, unlike scientists, most authors do not deal with subjects which are significantly cumulative, entailing consensual judgments of progress. A contribution in fiction does not directly build on what has been most recently written. What fellow authors write may stimulate thoughts, point to "hot" topics in the marketplace, and have a whole host of other influences; but by comparison to scientists, authors have far fewer inducements to establish regular and extensive personal contacts with their professional counterparts.[13]

Other differences in the external economies of cultural

realms are critical as well—in particular, how rewards are distributed. For scientists, peer evaluation assumes a central position in their professional lives. This evaluation determines who gets grants and fellowships, who is hired for jobs, and who is published in professional journals. Because judgment is passed on one's professional competence, self-esteem is inevitably affected. Since peer review is such an institutionalized feature of the scientific world, scientists have strong incentives to be professionally visible, to promote themselves to their colleagues.

The contrast with authors is obvious and sharp. Above all, their economic success is determined by the decisions of professional outsiders—in the first instance, publishers and, ultimately, the book-buying public. (At times, these outsiders may bring in authors to review nonfiction manuscripts, but their role is far less central and institutionalized than that of peer reviews in science.) In some cases honorific recognition is tied to the evaluation of a few prominent colleagues; but as Coser, Kadushin and Powell (1982) suggest, networks among authors generally have an insignificant role in bringing a writer's work to the favorable attention of publishers. The dust jacket comments of fellow authors have an indeterminate effect on sales and probably have more to do with the requests of publishers than personal ties between authors. In effect, little of a material sort hinges on peer evaluation for authors, although favorable reviews may bring some psychological compensation. The reward structure they confront thus provides little incentive for them to be connected.

Paralleling these differences in the technical and material incentives for collaboration are fundamental differences in the normative systems of science and authorship. Scientific norms not only encourage collaboration, but lead young scientists to participate openly in exchanging their ideas with colleagues. The normative structure of authorship may be quite different. Authors may believe that they should create alone, that they are encouraged, in fact, to make use of what Herbert Spencer called "cerebral hygiene," a form of self-imposed intellectual isolation from the works of others in order not to contaminate one's own originality. A significant proportion of authors may adopt this ancient medical practice, and may even avoid

Connections Among Authors

talking to others about their work lest they expend their creative energy in talking rather than in writing.

Differences in the external economics facing authors and scientists, then, may help explain the different degrees of connectedness among the producers of scientific and literary culture. In addition, perhaps the external economics to which elite intellectuals and artists are tied may induce some intermediate level of interaction. As a group, intellectuals have, of course, been usefully defined in different lights, but for our purposes we follow Kadushin's view of them as generalists who write about "values, morals, politics, and esthetics, not for specialists but for so-called educated laymen and, of course, each other" (1976:773). A much smaller group than authors, their influence and public role are not so exclusively restricted to books. Most academics do not assume this generalist role, even though many intellectuals have positions in academe.

Kadushin's (1974) research on this group supports the view that many intellectuals are quite densely connected to each other, much more so than authors, but the structure of scientific and elite intellectual circles appears to differ with the latter being not as generally extensive or "star-centered." In part this finding of substantial connections among prominent intellectuals is likely an artifact of the sampling procedures employed, but this sizable group of cultural producers seems to have distinctive patterns of interaction which set them apart from both academic scientists and authors, even the most esteemed.

This pattern is understandable in light of the external economy perspective. Coser has argued that intellectuals depend on each other for creative stimulation and idea-testing, though not for the actual production of ideas. He writes:

Despite popular myth to the contrary, most intellectuals cannot produce their work in solitude but need the give and take of debate and discussion with their peers in order to develop their ideas. Not all intellectuals are gregarious, but most of them need to test their own ideas in exchange with those they deem their equals. (1965:3-4)

Moreover, while the intellectual world does not have the fully institutionalized equivalent of peer evaluation, personal networks seem consequential in the allocation of review assignments, lectures, and the like—opportunities which provide public visibility and material reward.

The few existing studies on connections among artists suggest that, at least in particular locales, they may become intense. Analyses of both the Impressionists and abstract expressionists indicate that the social supports developed among artists were significant for the emergence of a new style. White and White, for instance, write: "The Impressionists' definition and solution of formal and technical problems was to some degree, then, a result of the social structure of their group and the circumstances of their work in partial isolation from the official system and its styles" (1965:118). But besides enhancing the flow of ideas and providing the emotional support of a group, connections with colleagues link painters to related circles of dealers, exhibitors, and critics—all crucial components of the art world's external economy (Rogers 1970; Rosenberg 1970).

Particularly as artists seek to explore new aesthetic terrain, the structural inducements for them to be linked to their counterparts seem significant, although probably less so than for scientists. The inducements which emerge in the art world would seem to affect a fairly small number (for example, those at the cutting edge of a new style), but very little reason exists to expect comparable inducements among any set of authors. Though necessarily speculative, such a line of reasoning suggests that a more detailed inquiry into the external economics of cultural realms may prove profitable in explaining their social organization.[14]

Finally, we ask directly, What are the consequences of this disconnectedness among authors? One implication seems clear: editors cannot readily tie into networks of authors as a quick way to drum up desirable manuscripts and screen out the undesirable or to stay current with emerging senses of taste and sharpen their own judgments. These tasks are all central to the editorial process, but authors are of small assistance. The informal social organization of authors is so diffuse that there is not much to which editors can efficiently connect. The difficulties of pursuing such a strategy are compounded by the surprisingly loose links within the publishing industry (Coser, Kadushin, and Powell 1982). Thus the informal social organization of two critical elements of the literary production process can do little to further the integration of the book industry.

How social organization among the producers affects the content and style of literary culture is an intriguing but unresolved issue. The breadth of the topic extends far beyond this research, and others are manifestly better equipped to assess the intellectual characteristics of our literature. However, we would like to discourage inferences of simple, mechanistic linkages between the general pattern of disconnectedness and some presumed character of American literature. Even if one assumes the importance of certain sorts of interpersonal relations for individual creative achievement—for intellectual stimulation, emotional support, and as a measure of accomplishment—one should not infer that American authors lack the necessary social integration to pursue the truly innovative or to collectively pursue in depth some common theme. However one may wish to characterize American literature, its degree of innovation and thematic concerns do not critically rest on general patterns of isolation among authors. What comes to be viewed as distinctive and consequential is created by relatively few. Some of them may deviate from the general lack of personal connections; others may find sufficient support and direction from the writings of their peers. Indeed, with the wide availability of books, authors may readily talk silently with each other, even if they do not fully recognize the significance of these conversations.

6.
Selected Portraits

> When I write, I aim in my mind not toward New York but toward a vague spot a little east of Kansas. I think of the books on library shelves, without their jackets, years old, and a countryish teen-aged boy finding them, and having them speak to him. The reviews, the stacks in Brentano's, are just hurdles to get over, to place the books on that shelf.
> John Updike

WHILE EMPHASIZING the diversity among authors in preceding chapters, we can sharpen our focus still further by briefly presenting collective portraits of certain groups. In these sketches we focus on occupational commitments and financial circumstances and also allude to any distinctive patterns of social and professional connections.[1]

Of course, many groups of authors share commitments, fates, and attributes that deserve special attention. We have limited our portraits to several groups of writers which seem to hold widespread interest. First, we consider three groups of authors who have widely divergent levels of financial success—the low-income writers, the modestly successful, and the best-sellers. Next we look at the young authors, the older authors, and women authors.

The Low-Income Writers: Authors who received $5,000 or less in 1979 from their writing.

If we begin by considering low-income authors as those who received less than $5,000 per year in writing-related income, our portrait will include more than half of all authors.[2] Aside from their common poor economic return to writing, they were a markedly diverse lot, which is apparent in several respects.

The ranks of the low-income earners were filled by authors with varying commitments to writing as an economic activity. Among our five types of authors, we find committed full-timers—21 percent, limited full-timers—21 percent, committed part-timers—11 percent, intermittent part-timers—27 percent, and marginal part-timers—20 percent. The low-income writers, therefore, do not all write as a relatively minor sidelight to some other career. More than 40 percent of the low-income writers spent on average twenty-five hours or more a week on their craft.

Low writing income was shared by authors across the whole range of writing genres. Of course, the predominance of writers primarily committed to adult nonfiction (25%) and adult fiction (19%) reflected the general concentration of authors within these genres, but notable numbers of academic writers (16%), children's book authors (15%), and genre fiction authors (10%) also suffered this fate. The rest of the low-income writers were primarily committed to the relatively uncommon genres—poetry, how-to-books, etc.

Even though the low-income writers did not have publication records as impressive as their better-off fellows, they were not an unproductive group. Some 60 percent had a book published within the period 1977 to early 1980, and more than 90 percent had a book published with the decade. Furthermore, from a career-long perspective, the low-income writers often had distinguished publication records. While 44 percent had only two or fewer books published, another 41 percent had three to nine books, and 14 percent actually had ten or more books to their credit. Both fledgling and veteran authors were thus represented within the ranks of low-income writers. Low writing

Selected Portraits

income is not some dues-paying fate borne only by those starting a career.

Diversity was also apparent in certain personal characteristics of the low-income writers. All ages were represented, with those fifty to sixty-four most common; their age distribution corresponded quite closely to the distribution for all authors. Their distribution by sex also mirrored the break-down for authors in general: about 60 percent men and 40 percent women.

What were these writers' attitudes toward the economic pay-off to their writing? In response to the question, "How significant are economic considerations for you in choosing among writing projects?" we found divergent viewpoints. Thirty-six percent considered them "decisive" or "important," a response suggesting that the low economic success of many did not reflect uncompromising aversion to being "commercial." And yet about an equal number considered economic considerations a "small concern" or "irrelevant." (The remaining fifth viewed economic considerations as of "some influence.") There is, of course, no reason to suppose that those who downplayed economic considerations in choosing projects objected to financial success.

Only a few of the low-income writers were so discouraged by their lack of financial success that they anticipated giving up writing. Further, the part-timers among this group generally preferred writing to their other job: some three-fifths found writing to be "much more" or "somewhat more" satisfying, while less than a tenth indicated such preference for their other job.[3]

For the most part, their low writing incomes did not represent a one-year aberration from a generally profitable career. Almost nine out of ten in the group had a similarly low return to their writing in 1978; only 4 percent earned more than $10,000 in the preceding year. Moreover, 42 percent had never made more than $5,000 annually from writing, and 64 percent had never exceeded $10,000 in any year. In short, very few of these writers could look back on high-income years.

Nevertheless, the median total personal income of this group was approximately $20,000, though about a quarter of them had personal incomes below $7,500. About half had family incomes in the top fifth of the national income distribution; a quarter, in the top 5 percent. The family incomes of approximately another fifth of these writers were in the second and third highest fifths of the national distribution (i.e., 40-80 percentiles). However, about a tenth of these authors had family incomes in the second lowest fifth (20-40 percentiles), and another tenth were in the lowest fifth; this latter group obviously endured considerable financial hardship. Finally, these low-income authors did not vary from the financially successful writers in "talking writing" with fellow authors or nonauthors, socializing frequently with their counterpart, or having many author friends.

The Modestly Successful: Authors who received $10,000 to $20,000 in 1979 from writing

In expressing his aspirations for writing income one highly praised novelist said; "I aim for $15,000; an author should be able to live on that." With diverse occupational commitments to writing, 13 percent of authors attained about this modest level. They were predominantly committed (43%) and limited full-time (18%) authors, but substantial numbers were part-timers: committed (12%), intermittent (19%), and marginal (8%). Compared to the low-income writers, the proportion of full-timers was relatively large, but an undivided occupational commitment to writing was clearly not a prerequisite for attaining this level of financial success.

Like their low income counterparts, the modestly successful authors worked in diverse genres, though again adult nonfiction (27 percent of the group), children's books (19%), and adult fiction (14%) were most common. Also within the ranks of the modestly successful were significant numbers of genre fiction authors (10%) and how-to book writers (11%). Academic writers and poets, two groups that generally write without any real prospect of financial gain, had a much lower representation than their proportion in the total sample.

A significant proportion (39%) of authors earning modest incomes had been very productive with ten or more books to their

Selected Portraits

credit, but a modest or limited publication record did not preclude an author from attaining this income level. Twenty-seven percent had five to nine books, another 16 percent had three or four books, and 19 percent had published one or two books.[4] Since writing income is so dependent on royalties from recent books, it is not surprising that more than 80 percent of these modestly successful writers had had a book published within the last three years.

The modestly successful were diverse in age, with no age group disproportionally represented. About 60 percent were men, 40 percent women—proportions that matched the general distribution of authors.

Almost all these authors expected to continue writing, but they voiced varied attitudes about the importance of economic considerations in choosing among writing projects. Twenty-three percent viewed these considerations as "decisive" and another 31 percent as "important," while 23 percent saw them as having "some influence," 11 percent as "a small concern," and 13 percent as "irrelevant." When asked, "How frequently have you given up the personally most interesting project in favor of one that promised greater sales?" we received the following answers: 22 percent said "often"; another 27 percent, "occasionally"; 9 percent, "once"; and 42 percent said "never." One author offered what appeared to be a widespread view about the tension between the pursuit of personal interests and commercial success. "I try to have it both ways. I try to write the best book I can but really hope it can sell. I want it to be read and try to write an appealing book."

Since about 40 percent of the modestly successful were part-timers, it is worth noting that about three-fifths considered writing to be "much more" or "somewhat more" satisfying than their other job. Only a few percent indicated any actual preference for their other job. Although these modestly successful part-timers generally preferred writing, their level of success apparently did not create a distinctly strong preference for it. The part-timers among the low-income writers had very similar views on the relative appeal of writing and other jobs.

Although these authors earned enough from writing to support themselves in a very modest way, most of them drew on other sources of income. Their median personal income reached $26,000; about two-thirds had family incomes in the top fifth of the national income distribution, and more than half of them were in the top 5 percent.[5] However, at least as notable is that almost a quarter of these highly trained writers had family incomes which placed them *below* the sixtieth percentile in the national income distribution.

The Best-Sellers: Authors whose work appeared on the New York Times best-seller lists in 1978 or 1979

With multimillion dollar advances receiving wide attention, a number of best-selling authors have become celebrities and the subjects of media attention. Yet, as we have emphasized, there is no reason to see any resemblance between the monetary success of the relatively few best-sellers and the vast number of authors. The distribution of financial rewards in writing is highly skewed: a few earn a great deal, and the large majority receive very little. If the total writing income in 1979 was distributed equally among the individuals who met our inclusive definition of an author, each would have received more than $21,000. Instead, the typical writer (as indicated by the median) received less than $5,000.

About 3 percent of the authors in our survey had a book on one of the *New York Times* best seller lists in 1978 or 1979. Of the authors with a book published in that period, the percentage of best-sellers reached 4.5.

Obviously authors of best-sellers received substantial, financial gains, but we can provide only a somewhat questionable estimate of their typical earnings. Their median writing-related income in 1979 was $109,000. Since their best-sellers had been so recently published, not all earnings had been received by 1979, and thus we probably underestimated the typical monetary reward for writing a best-seller. Nevertheless, even allowing for this, the million dollar deals which receive such publicity represent the good fortune of a minute proportion of authors who write best-sellers.

The writing careers of authors of best-sellers during this period suggest that their great success did not emerge as a sudden stroke of good fortune. More than three-quarters of them were more than forty years old, and the great majority had a considerable record of publications: 73 percent had at least five books to their credit, and only about 15 percent had made a best-seller list with one of their first two books. Furthermore, the best-selling authors then were apt to have been best-sellers in the past. About half of the authors on the best-seller lists in 1978 or 1979 had been on one of the lists at some prior time.

Not surprisingly, given their great financial success, the large majority (83%) of the best-sellers were full-timers, but few were inclined to follow a relaxed writing schedule. The overwhelming number (88%) usually wrote at least twenty hours per week, and 44 percent averaged at least forty hours.

By their own accounts, their success could not be attributed to some distinctly great commerical-mindedness. When asked how frequently they had "given up or postponed the personally most interesting project in favor of one that promised greater sales?" most of them responded "never." Indeed, their responses suggested a slight tendency to be less commercially minded than all other authors. Similarly, when asked to rate the significance of economic considerations in choosing among writing projects, they were more likely than the others to say it was "a small concern" or "irrelevant." We certainly cannot discount the possibility that these successful authors were responding normatively, that is, that they felt they ought to be motivated by noncommercial reasons and responded accordingly. Furthermore, we do not know whether this response reflects the fact that their economic success allowed them to consider noncommercial writing options, but they certainly did not avow a distinctive concern for money.

Indeed, the secret of writing a best-seller seems elusive, even if a very few writers appear on the lists year after year. As one author of best-sellers of the late fifties and early sixties said in an interview: "It's always hard work. There's no 'formula' to fall back on." Perhaps it is not always true, as he claims, that "people don't really care what you've done in the past," but having once been a best-seller is no guarantee of a continuing spot at the top of the lists.

The financial success of these best-sellers was not accompanied by any tendency to engage or shun fellow authors. Some were occupationally connected, but most are not in any intense way.

The Young

Young writers, men and women under thirty, were a rarity—less than 2 percent of all authors. In light of their thin ranks, a limitation in our sample becomes particularly clear: only published book writers met our definition of an author.[6] Yet, undoubtedly, there are substantial numbers of young people, supporting themselves in a variety of ways, who are trying to break into print. One highly praised novelist recounted that she received many "good" manuscripts from young authors, but requests for literary advice were usually secondary to a plea for help in becoming published. Because these pleas often seemed "desperate," she worried that many talented writers had given up in discouragement. Clearly, the fate of these unpublished writers should be of concern, but we can report on only those who made it over the considerable hurdle of a first publication. Moreover, since there were only twenty-nine authors under thirty in the survey, our portrait of young authors must be drawn with tentativeness.

Although the large majority had only one publication, the young authors in our sample were particularly likely to be single-minded in their commitment to writing; more than two-thirds were full-timers. (Fifty-five percent of all authors were full-timers.) Whether such a high proportion would decide to continue full time was, of course, an open question, but their typical economic return to writing was not likely to be a major inducement to do so. Only about half earned more than $5,050 in writing income in 1979; their median hourly wage for writing was $3.67. These figures were quite comparable to those of their older counterparts.

But also like the older authors, they generally had substantial personal resources on which to draw, especially education. More than 90 percent had attained at least a bachelor's degree. These young authors could significantly augment their generally low writing-related earnings with income from decently paying other jobs, irregular and regular—they were not living off unearned income. Their typical total personal income was nonetheless a very modest $13,038. Clearly, the prevailing pattern by which authors subsidize their writing by compensation from other sources held for young authors as well.

Being a newcomer to the occupation did not mean that they led distinctly isolated professional lives, though by comparison to older writers, the young authors had slightly smaller networks among colleagues. Apparently they were not discouraged by their existence because they all expected to continue writing.

The Older Writers

One might expect that the economic fate of older writers—the 17 percent of all authors who were sixty-five or more—to be of particular concern because only those with lengthy service in other jobs could count on substantial private pension benefits and Social Security. Many of the older writers were still active as authors and in their other jobs; but by the age of sixty-five, income from other employment has generally fallen off, and the necessary energies for writing may be expected to decline as well. Nevertheless, though many may have lacked substantial private or public retirement coverage, the older writers typically had a moderate standard of living. Their median total family income was $30,000; however, about a tenth—all with incomes below $9,000—were hard-pressed financially.

Writing-related income was generally relatively unimportant to their economic condition (the median writing income was $2,500). But their low return to writing did not simply represent a reduced work schedule. On an hourly basis, older writers typically earned only $3.00. The median income derived from their investments, pensions, and Social Security reached $12,000; and this income typically represented just less than half of their total family income.

Although we are considering a group that is past the usual

retirement age in most companies, the older writers were not an economically inactive group. Of the full-timers within this sample (82 percent of the total), committed full-timers were only slightly outnumbered by limited full-timers.[7] Not surprisingly, the older authors tended to have published more books than their younger counterparts, but ongoing commitment to writing was evidenced by the fact that slightly more than half had brought out a book in the years 1977–1980. (More than 80 percent had published at least one book in the 1970s.) Furthermore, almost nine out of ten older authors expected to continue writing, inspite of the low financial rewards.

The thought of facing retirement without pension provisions weighed heavily in the career decisions of some authors. One older author who had written on a full-time basis but was now closing in on age sixty-five was "greatly relieved" to be offered a job, not only because the job was interesting but also because it offered the chance to get better retirement benefits. How typical he was we do not know. Yet, as he recognized, the general prospects of living off past or future writing income were dim.

Old age tended to exacerbate slightly the disconnectedness of authors. As a group, they were not all professional isolates, but were somewhat less likely to talk writing with fellow authors (or others) or to socialize with them. Thus, almost four-fifths of them (79%) met socially with other writers no more than every few months as compared to 68 percent of all younger writers. Their social and professional networks were also slightly smaller than those of their younger colleagues. Of course, none of this is really surprising; reduced social contacts often go along with old age. More remarkable was the occupational vitality of so many.

Women Authors

As part of a general concern about women's social contributions, women authors and their work have been singled out for special attention in books, essays, press reports, and university courses.

Selected Portraits

Women represent 40 percent of all authors in this sample. Many of them wrote before a recognizable women's movement materialized, and it is fair to say that the great majority did not write on self-consciously feminist themes.

With regard to their writing careers, female authors were certainly not alike; there were simply too many with diverse involvements in writing to present a typical female author. We will show their differences and commonalities in the following portrait; but since women authors are partly of interest insofar as they differ from men authors, we will also note similarities and differences between the sexes.

Author Type. Female authors clearly varied in their commitments to writing as an economic activity. About two-thirds of the female authors were full-timers, and more than half were committed full-timers. Yet significant numbers also held regular other jobs, and depending on their time commitment to writing could thus be typed as committed part-timers (10%), intermittent part-timers (15%), and marginal part-timers (11%).

Compared to their male counterparts, female authors were somewhat more likely to be full-timers, especially limited full-timers, but this disparity was primarily attributable to the difference between the married male and married female authors. Among the single and divorced authors the occupational commitment to writing only slightly differed between the sexes. By contrast, among the married authors the proportion of women with full-time status was pronounced: 38 percent of the women were committed full-timers, and 28 percent were limited full-timers, while the respective figures for men were 31 percent and 13 percent. Undoubtedly, this difference among the married authors largely reflects the fact that women typically bear the prime responsibility for child-rearing and housework in their families. This responsibility often precludes them from holding another job; and once at home, the time involved in raising children often leaves only a limited opportunity for writing. As one housewife-author wrote to us: "What I desire above all is time to write. People don't realize how difficult it is [for the housewife] to find uninterrupted time for writing."

Genre. The women authors were also diverse in what they wrote, as indicated by their broad dispersion across our eleven categories of writing genre. They most commonly (25%) composed children's literature, but comparable numbers devoted themselves primarily to adult nonfiction (18%) and general adult fiction (20%). Moreover, almost all differences between the sexes in their commitments to particular genres were remarkably slight, with the only notable exception being children's literature. Women authors were almost three times more likely to write mainly in this genre than men (25 percent versus 9 percent).

Income. As we observed in chapter 4, about half of the female and male authors received less than $5,000 in writing related income in 1979. About 30 percent of the women earned more than $10,000; only 7 percent had distinctly high ($50,000+) incomes from writing. Although male authors were somewhat more likely than the female authors to be financially successful through their writing, the overwhelming number of authors of both sexes were clearly unable to support themselves by publication. The 1979 median writing-related income among women authors was $4,000; for the men it was $5,200. Given these low levels, their common poverty as writers was perhaps more noteworthy than their differences in income.[8]

Nonetheless, the median total family income in 1979 among women authors was $39,000, and only a tenth had family incomes below $9,370. Obviously, their typical contributions to family income through writing were minor (13%), and they had to count on money from their husband's and their own other jobs as their prime means of support.

Recognition. Were women authors less apt than men to receive recognition for their writing? Our limited indicators suggest the differences were fairly slight. Women authors were somewhat less likely to be reviewed in the *New York Times Book Review* in 1978 or 1979 than were men (20 percent and 26 percent, respectively). However, virtually equal proportions of men and women authors had been reviewed in this prominent publication at some time in previous years. Furthermore, women were as apt as men to have written a best-seller in 1978 or 1979, though men were more likely than women to have had a best-seller in earlier years—11 percent versus 7 percent. Women authors had also had their share of honorific awards; almost half had received at least one award, just slightly less than the proportion among men.

Occupational integration. It is simple to discuss the occupational integration of female authors because they did not have distinctive patterns of social or professional connections with their professional peers. Within the limited scope of this survey, women authors' views about writing also did not set them apart from men. The overwhelming majority of men and women authors expected to continue writing, and both groups showed a fairly restrained concern for maximizing their economic return to writing. To the question whether they had "given up or postponed the personally most interesting (writing) project in favor of one that promised greater sales," about 60 percent of each sex reported having done so only "once" or "never." An equally small proportion of each reported that they did so "often." Only a small number of authors, male or female, reported that economic considerations were "decisive" in choosing among writing projects.

Among the part-timers, men and women did not differ significantly in their motivation for holding additional jobs. About half of each saw their other jobs simply as a means for "necessary income for living." Of all these writers with other jobs, a clear majority of the men and women alike considered writing to be "much more" or "somewhat more" satisfying than their other work.

Female and male authors, then, approached writing in a markedly similar way: they both had an ongoing commitment to writing, reported only a moderate calculation of economic return in choosing projects, and generally preferred writing to other jobs. Indeed, several women authors whom we interviewed strongly suggested that one should not expect any differences—particularly that women are any less serious about their writing than men. One commented: "I work hard at writing, at writing the best book I can and resent the fact that some people somehow think because I'm a woman writing children's books that what I do is not serious.... It's hard work." Another female novelist remarked: "Look, I'm interested in writing good books. I'm not interested in being a good 'woman author.'"

This survey and set of interviews cannot tell us the extent to which women authors have faced sex discrimination in their careers, nor even the extent to which they believed they had suffered from discrimination. Except for a few passing remarks, the female respondents simply did not raise the issue. Yet if the several women we interviewed were representative of women authors generally, divided opinion existed on this issue. An older woman simply said, " I've had no trouble being a woman," and this view was largely echoed by a younger author. By contrast, a female novelist believed that women receive disproportionately low advances and poor publicity compared to men. Our data cannot speak to this claim, but quite clearly many authors, both men and women, thought that they had been victimized in these ways.

Coda

OUR MAIN FINDINGS were presented as a series of headlines in the introductory chapter and do not bear repeating here, but some final remarks about the limitations and implications of the study are in order.

Recall our primary intention to explore the concerns suggested by Robert Benchley's view of the freelance writer as "one who gets paid per word, per piece, or perhaps." By no means, however, should this statistical focus on the "job-side" of being a writer deflect attention from the fact that authors are vital creators of culture. They define and sharpen our range of knowledge and awareness of ignorance, our values, and our commitments—both personal and social. Of course, this is a task to which authors make varying contributions, and yet their collective contribution is undeniably distinct and significant. In our view, both the "job" and creative sides of being a writer deserve attention, as does the relationship between the two. Practical, policy-oriented concerns in addition to theoretical issues emerge about this relationship.

For the most part, American society supports literature through the decisions of the marketplace. As our study made plain, this support does not typically provide a living wage, and few receive even a modest income from writing. Necessarily, most authors must be subsidized; other jobs and spouses are the modern-day patrons of our literature. Not often providing affluence, these sources generally provide the wherewithal for at least modest material comfort. But the obvious inadequacy of market support for writing raises the issue of appropriate public response. Should authors be publicly subsidized, and if so in what ways?

Answers to these questions depend on personal values—that is, matters outside the purview of social science—as well as judgments on empirical matters about which we know little. Specifically, no amount of research can show that authors deserve more support, and no one can say with any confidence how authors' economic circumstances affect the character of our literature (though most authors in our study do not report great concern about marketability in selecting what to write about). Would lesser worry about financial matters induce more talented people to write, or encourage more ambitious, innovative works with relatively low commercial promise? People may have different convictions about what would occur, but they all lack good evidence.

We believe that our data provide valuable contextual information for debates about what should be done and what are the best ways to advance certain goals. For example, interest has arisen recently in instituting a policy whereby authors would in some way be recompensed for the use of their books in public libraries. The experience of Great Britain and other countries shows that such policies can be manageable and quite inexpensive. We advance no brief here for the idea in general or for specific proposals, but any discussion about the need or value of such an initiative should be informed by a systematic awareness of the economic condition of authors.

We were also largely silent about the connection between the economic and social circumstances of authors and the character of our literary culture. For instance, how does the class position of authors affect what and how they write? How does the generally diffuse social organization among authors affect patterns of innovation, thematic focus and consistency, and stylistic evolution? Such questions go to the classic core of the sociology of knowledge—the relationship between social structure and ideas. They are much easier to raise than to answer; sociological progress has been limited. At the same time,

Coda

any attempt to develop compelling answers must be firmly based on knowledge of the social position of the "cultural producers"—in literature and other realms.

Yet if the relationship between the job and creative sides of writing creates tensions for public policy and sociological theory, they are most acutely felt by authors themselves. If it is indeed true, as Samuel Johnson told us, that "no one but a blockhead ever wrote except for money," contemporary authors are either collectively blind to their economic reality or blockheads are in great supply.

We thankfully see a continuing supply even if we have removed some blindness.

Appendix A

Reproductions of the Questionnaires and Accompanying Cover Letters

THE AUTHORS GUILD FOUNDATION, INC.
234 WEST 44TH STREET, NEW YORK, N.Y. 10036 • (212) 398-0838

Dear Colleague:

We have commissioned the Center for the Social Sciences at Columbia University to do a professional study of the economic condition of authors in the United States. We hope to correct whatever distorted ideas people may have about writers' incomes. Authors themselves, many of them, have only a limited perspective on the careers of others in their own profession. We expect that the study will provide an accurate up-to-date body of fact.

We need your help. Your name was selected either from The Authors Guild membership list or from a separate list of authors who are not members of the Guild. We urge you to complete the enclosed questionnaire. It should not take more than a few minutes of your time. We are depending on your cooperation and that of several thousand other writers to preserve the integrity of the sample.

Appendix A: Questionnaires

The survey asks for information that most people consider private, but we can assure you that, as the enclosed letter indicates, the Columbia research center will treat all replies with strict concern for your privacy.

We want this study to present a realistic picture of the economic condition of authors. You can help to make the survey effective by completing the enclosed questionnaire and sending it on to Columbia, as soon as you can. Many thanks.

Sincerely,

Peter S. Prescott
President

Officers
President: PETER S. PRESCOTT
Vice President: ELIZABETH JANEWAY   Secretary: HOWARD TAUBMAN
Treasurer: TONI MORRISON

Members Of The Board

JOHN BROOKS	ELIZABETH JANEWAY	SIDNEY OFFIT
ROBERT A. CARO	EVE MERRIAM	PETER S. PRESCOTT
BRUCE BLIVEN, JR.	HERBERT MITGANG	NANCY WILSON ROSS
MADELEINE L'ENGLE	TONI MORRISON	HOWARD TAUBMAN

Appendix A: Questionnaires

Columbia University in the City of New York | *New York*, N.Y. 10027
CENTER FOR THE SOCIAL SCIENCES   420 West 118th Street

Dear Author:

On the request of the Authors Guild Foundation, we have designed a questionnaire to elicit information about the economic circumstances of authors. If we receive a sufficient number of completed questionnaires, it will truly provide the necessary data for the first accurate protrait of authors' economic circumstances. We would be able to report on authors in general as well as on specific types. Since this survey is so promising, we would like to reiterate Peter Prescott's request for your cooperation.

In considering the survey questions, you will find most of them to be straightforward. We recognize that none of the responses to a few questions may fully reflect your own experience—this is an inevitable problem with surveys—but we ask you to check the response that best approximates your situation or attitude. In addition, we welcome any written comments explaining your answers or raising other issues. Your comments will certainly be taken into account in our reports.

Without qualification, we assure the confidentiality of your responses. No names will ever appear on any questionnaire, computer tape, working paper, or finished report. The names of those in the sample, known only to the project staff at the Center for the Social Sciences, will be destroyed immediately after the final mailing. Each person in the sample has been assigned a number which appears on the survey form (so that we may prompt those not responding to our first request), but this name-number list is locked away and available only to the project staff. It will also be destroyed after the last mailing. We are providing this detail to assure you of our professional commitment to protecting your confidentiality.

Of course you have the option of not answering particular questions. Should you not wish to respond to some questions, we hope that you will still complete the rest of the questionnaire.

Sincerely,

Jonathan R. Cole   Paul W. Kingston
Director   Research Associate

Appendix A: Questionnaires

Columbia University in the City of New York | *New York*, N.Y. 10027
CENTER FOR THE SOCIAL SCIENCES   420 West 118th Street

Dear Author:

Because your response is critical for the success of the Survey of American Authors, we are contacting you for a second time to ask for your help.

For the results of our study to be accurate, we need a high "response rate" from our randomly selected list of authors. (Part-time writers should know that we are very interested in their responses, no matter how little time they spend writing or how little money they earn from it.) Your cooperation can help us provide the first systematic portrait of the economic condition of authors. In writing our report, we will detail the economic conditions of authors in general, as well as the economic conditions of specific types of authors.

Without qualification, we assure you that your responses will be totally confidential. In the previous mailing each selected author was assigned a number for the sole purpose of allowing us to identify those who did not respond to our first request. However, we have not attached any identifying numbers to the enclosed questionnaire. Your response will therefore be completely anonymous.

In considering the survey questions, you will find most of them to be straightforward. We recognize that none of the responses to a few questions may fully reflect your own experience—this is an inevitable problem with surveys—but we ask you to check the response that best approximates your situation or attitude. In addition, we welcome any written comments explaining your answers or raising other issues. Your comments will certainly be taken into account in our reports.

Of course you have the option of not answering particular questions. Should you not wish to respond to some questions, we hope that you will still complete the rest of the questionnaire.

Sincerely,

Jonathan R. Cole   Paul W. Kingston
Director   Research Associate

Appendix A: Questionnaires

Center for the Social Sciences
Survey of American Authors

I. Occupation
   1. Would you characterize your occupation as full-time freelance author or writer?
      Yes ____₁   No ____₂   11
   2. On average, in the last year how many hours per week did you spend writing or directly working in some other way on your own book or article?
      Hours/week ____   12–13
   3. On average, in the last year how many hours per week did you work in a paying activity besides book or article writing? (Count regular and irregular work.)
      Hours/week ____   14–15
   4. In 1979 did you give any paid lectures or readings or do any irregular fee-for-service editing, translating, etc.?
      Yes ____₁   No ____₂   16
   5. Do you now hold a paid position besides freelance writing? (Do not count occasional lectures or readings or irregular fee-for-service editing, translating, etc.)
      Yes ____₁   No ____₂   17

Questions 6 and 7 should be answered only by authors who hold a paid position besides freelance writing. All others should skip to question 8.

6. What kind of paid position do you hold besides freelance writing? (If you hold more than one type of position, indicate the one from which you earn the most income.) 18–19

   ___₁ University teaching   ___₅ Primary/secondary teaching   ___₉ Public relations

   ___₂ Editor/publisher   ___₆ Clerical/secretarial   ___₁₀ Other professional

   ___₃ Manager/proprietor   ___₈ Sales/technical   ___₁₁ Other: specify _____

6a. Do you consider this a relatively permanent type of position for you? 20

   Yes ___₁   Possibly ___₂   No ___₃

7. Have you ever been a full-time writer for at least a year? 21

   ___₁ Yes   ___₂ No

7a. *If yes*: Indicate which years: _____ 22–36

Questions 8–10 should be answered only by authors who do *not* hold a paid position besides freelance writing.

---

8. For how many years have you been a full-time freelance writer? ___ Years 37–38

9. Since the end of your formal schooling, how many years have you primarily supported yourself by income from a position besides freelance writing? ___ Years 54–55

10. What type of position did you have immediately before becoming a full-time freelance writer? (If you held more than one job, indicate the one from which you earned the most income.)

   ___₁ None   ___₅ Manager/proprietor   ___₉ Public relations

   ___₂ Primary or secondary teaching   ___₆ Sales/clerical   ___₁₀ Other professional

   ___₃ University teaching   ___₇ Clerical/secretarial   ___₁₁ Other: specify _____

   ___₄ Editor/publisher   ___₈ Blue collar/service

Appendix A: Questionnaires

II. Income

Please provide your *best estimate* of the amount (pretax) that you received in each of the following categories for the calendar years 1978 and 1979. *We do not expect you to check your financial records.*

N.B. All income earned for salaried employment, *even if it involves writing* (e.g., newspaper reporter, editor, writing teacher), should be included in line 3, "Income from salaried employment." If you received no money in a particular category, mark a "0." Please do not simply leave it blank.

Round all figures to thousands	1978 Calendar year	1979 Calendar year
1. *Income directly related to writing*		
A. *Books*		
1. Royalties hardcover editions	_____58–63	_____141–146
2. Royalties paperback originals	_____64–69	_____147–152
3. Royalties paperback reprints	_____70–75	_____153–158
4. All subsidiary rights	_____76–81	_____159–164
5. Total income from books (sum of 1A1–1A4)	_____82–87	_____165–170
B. *Magazine and newspaper articles* (not reprints of books)	_____88–92	_____171–176
C. *Motion pictures/television/radio* (not including subsidiary rights in published books)	_____93–98	_____177–182
D. *Total income directly related to writing* (sum of 1A5, 1B, and 1C)	_____99–104	_____183–188
2. *Income from other freelance writing work* (lecturing, reading, consulting, editing, translating, etc.)	_____105–110	_____189–194
3. Income from salaried employment	_____111–115	_____195–200
4. *Income from investments/pensions/Social Security* (include income from investments jointly held with spouse)	_____117–122	_____201–206

5. Total *personal income*
(sum of 1D, 2, 3, and 4) ———123–128   ———207–212

6. *Spouse's income*
(all personal income, including ———129–134   ———213–218
income from investments sepa-
rately held)

7. Total family income
(sum of 5 and 6) ———135–140   ———219–224

8. Please provide your best estimate of the most, and the least, income that you have derived from *one book* (including all subsidiary rights) throughout your career.
    Most $———225–230   Least $———231–236

9. In what year did you earn the most writing-related income?   237–238
    19——
    9a. Indicate the amount: $————   239–245

10. Indicate the source(s) of any grants for writing that you
    have received in the past five years.   246
    ———₁Public agency   ———₂Both public and private   247
                                                sources
    ———₃Private foundation   ———₄Haven't received any

11. Do you have an agent?   ——— Yes₁   ——— No₂

12. What was the largest advance you ever received for a book?
    ———
    12a. How much of an advance did you receive from your
    last book? $———

III. Attitudes Toward Work
  1. Do you expect to continue writing?   260
     ——₁Yes   ——₂No   ——₃Unsure
  2. In choosing among ideas for books, how frequently have   261
     you given up or postponed the personally most interesting
     project in favor of one that promised greater sales:
         ——₁Often ——₂Occasionally ——₃Once ——₄Never

Appendix A: Questionnaires

Comments: _____

3. How significant are economic considerations for you now in choosing among writing projects?   262
   ___₁ Decisive ___₂Important ___₃Some influence ___₄A small concern ___₅Irrelevant
   Comments: _____

> Questions 4–6 should be answered only by authors who have paying work (regular or irregular) besides book or article writing. All others should skip to the next section.

4. What is your *primary* motivation for having paying work besides book or article writing (Check one.)   263
   ___₁Necessary income for living
   ___₂A desirable, complementary source of income
   ___₃Both complementary income and nonmonetary satisfaction
   ___₄Derive most work-related satisfaction from this other work
   ___₅Do not like writing full time
   ___₆Other: specify _____

5. How do you evaluate the personal satisfaction of writing as compared to your other work?   264
   ___₁Other job much more satisfying
   ___₂Writing much more satisfying
   ___₃About equally satisfying
   ___₄Other job somewhat more satisfying
   ___₅Writing somewhat more satisfying
   ___₆Not sure

6. If you could at least match your present total income by writing full time, would you drop your other work?   265
   ___₁Yes ___₂Possibly ___₃No ___₄Don't know

IV. Writing Activity
   1. How many books have you published? _____   266–267
      1a. Of this total, how many were fiction? ___₂₆₈₋₂₆₉
      poetry?___₂₇₀₋₂₇₁ ___nonfiction? ___₂₇₂₋₂₇₃

Appendix A: Questionnaires

2. List below the publication date, publisher, and *approximate* number of copies sold for your (a) last book, (b) first book, and (c) biggest selling book. Also, check whether each book is fiction/poetry or nonfiction.

	Year of publication	Publisher	Copies sold Hardcover	Paperback	Type Fiction/poetry	Nonfiction	
Last book:	19___274–275	___276	___277–282	___283–288	___1	___2	289
First book:	19___290–291	___292	___293–298	___299–304	___1	___2	305
Biggest seller:	19___306–307	___308	___309–314	___315–320	___1	___2	321

3. Do you currently belong to the Authors Guild? 322
   ___Yes₁   ___No₂

4. Have any of your books been reviewed in the *New York Times* 323
   Book Review in 1978 or 1979?
   ___Yes₁   ___No₂
   4a. At any other time in the past?   ___Yes₁ ___No₂   324

5. Did you have a book on one of the *New York Times* best-seller lists (i.e., one of the top fifteen positions on the fiction or nonfiction hardcover lists or the mass or trade paperback lists) at any time in 1978 or 1979?
   ___Yes₁   ___No₂   325
   5a. At any other time in the past?   ___Yes₁ ___No₂   326

6. List all awards (including nominations for awards) that you 327
   have received for your writing. ___None
   _____
                                                              328
   _____

7. What *single* category best describes the type of books to which you have given the most and second most time in your writing career?

Type of book	Most time spent on (check one):	Second most time spent on (check one):
"Genre fiction" (e.g., westerns, thrillers, mysteries, science fiction, historical romances, and gothic/occult novels)	___1	___1
General adult fiction	___2	___2
Academically oriented nonfiction	___3	___3

Appendix A: Questionnaires

Adult nonfiction (e.g., current events; popularizations of history, science, psychology, etc.; and biographies)	_____₄	_____₄
"How-to" books (sex, gardening, cooking, etc.) or travel guides	_____₅	_____₅
Technical reports/manuals/ textbooks	_____₆	_____₆
Poetry	_____₇	_____₇
Children's books	_____₈	_____₈
Religious/inspirational	_____₉	_____₉
Translations	_____₁₀	_____₁₀
Other	_____₁₁	_____₁₁
	No secondary type of publication	_____₁₂
	329–330	331–332

V. Basic Background Matters
1. Your sex: ___₁Male ___₂Female   2. Your age:___   333
   334–335
3. Your highest educational attainment: 336
   ___₁Less than a high-school degree ___₂High-school degree
   ___₃Some college ___₄B.A./B.S. ___₅M.A. (arts and science)
   ___₆Professional degree ___₇Ph.D.
4. If you at least attended college, write out the name of your   337
   undergraduate school. (Do not abbreviate.)
   _____
5. Your marital status: ___₁Single ___₂Married ___₃Divorced or   338
   separated
6. Number of children: ___   339
7. Your predominant religious background: 340
   ___₁Roman Catholic ___₂Jewish ___₃Protestant ___₄Other
   ___₅None
8. Your race: 341
   ___₁White ___₂Black ___₃Asian ___₄Hispanic ___₅Other
9. Did either of your parents or any close relatives ever publish   342
   a book?
            ___₁Yes   ___₂No .

10. Your father's main type of work while you were in high school: 343
    ___₁Educator ___₂Author ___₃Other professional
    ___₄Clerical/sales/ technical ___₅Blue collar/ service ___₆Manager/ proprietor
    ___₇Other: specify___

11. Highest educational attainment of your better-educated parent: 344
    ___₁Less than high school ___₂High school
    ___₃Some college ___₄B.A./B.S. ___₅Post-college degree

12. Your spouse's main type of work now: 345–346
    ___₁Freelance author ___₂Publisher/editor ___₃Homemaker
    ___₄Journalist ___₅Manager/ proprietor ___₆Clerical/sales/ technical
    ___₇Blue collar/ service ___₈Educator ___₉Other professional
    ___₁₀Retired ___₁₁Other: specify ___

13. Primary area of residence: 347
    ___₁New York metropolitan area ___₂South ___₃California
    ___₄Other Northeast ___₅Midwest ___₉Other West

VI. Connections with Other Authors
   1. Do you seriously discuss ideas for books or work in progress with other authors?
      ___₁Always ___₂Usually ___₃Sometimes ___₄Never 348
      1a. With how many authors did you seriously discuss your most recent work? ___ 349
      1b. How have these discussions affected your work? ___
      ___
   2. Besides your relatives, do you seriously discuss ideas for books or work with people who are not authors?
      ___₁Always ___₂Usually ___₃Sometimes ___₄Never 350
   3. How often do you meet with other authors in some social setting? (Exclude your spouse.)
      ___₁At least once a week ___₂At least once a month 351
      ___₃Every few months ___₄Rarely

Appendix A: Questionnaires

5. Of the three contemporary authors who have most significantly influenced your own writing, what is the closest relationship you have?
   ___₁None has significantly influenced my work
   ___₂"Know" him or her only through published writing
   ___₃Have had some conversations
   ___₄Friendly acquaintanceship
   ___₅Friend
   ___₆Other: specify. _____

Comments:
    If you desire, please write any comments below. We welcome comments explaining your responses to our questions or raising additional issues related to your career, including proposals to improve the economic circumstances of writers.

Appendix A: Questionnaires

Columbia University in the City of New York | New York, N.Y. 10027
CENTER FOR THE SOCIAL SCIENCES   420 West 118th Street

June 2, 1980

Dear Author:
      As part of our effort to produce an accurate study of American authors for the Authors Guild, we are contacting a number of randomly selected Guild members who apparently have not responded to our first mailing.
      To check the validity of our findings, we want to see whether "nonrespondents" differ from the "respondents" in certain respects. We hope that you will help us and take a minute or so to answer the few questions on the other side of this page.
      N.B. If you have already completed a questionnaire, please indicate so on the first question of this questionnaire. This issue arises because we have no way of knowing the names of those who responded to the second mailing.
      We cannot identify the names of those responding to this "mini-questionnaire," and thus your confidentiality is absolutely guaranteed.
      Your brief cooperation can significantly improve the quality of this study.
      Thank you.

                        Sincerely,

                        Paul Kingston
                        Project Director

Center for the Social Sciences
Survey of American Authors

1. Have you previously completed an American Authors questionnaire?
                Yes___   No___
(*If yes*: Please send us the questionnaire, anyway. There is no need to complete the rest of this page.)

2. Would you characterize your occupation as a full-time freelance author or writer?
                Yes___   No___

3. How many books have you had published? _____

4. Did you have a book published in 1978, 1979, or 1980?   Yes___ No___

5. Have any of your books been reviewed in the *New York Times Book Review* in 1978 or 1979?
                Yes___   No___
   5a. At any other time in the past?   Yes___ No___

Appendix A: Questionnaires

6. Did you have a book on one of the *New York Times* best-seller lists (i.e., one of the top fifteen positions on the fiction or nonfiction hardcover lists or the mass or trade paperback lists) at any time in 1978 or 1979?
                   Yes___   No___

   6a. At any other time in the past?   Yes___   No___

7. Please provide your best *estimate of your 1979 income directly related to books.* Include all royalties (and advances) and all subsidiary rights.
   - ___ $0–$2,499
   - ___ $2,5000–$4,999
   - ___ $5,000–$9,999
   - ___ $10,000–$19,999
   - ___ $20,000–$49,999
   - ___ $50,000–$99,999
   - ___ $100,000 or more

8. Your age:_____

9. What *single* category best describes the type of books to which you have given the most time in your writing career?

Type of book	Most time spent on (check one):
"Genre fiction" (e.g., westerns, thrillers, mysteries, science fiction, historical romances, and gothic/occult novels)	_____
General adult fiction	_____
Academically oriented nonfiction	_____
Adult nonfiction (e.g., current events; popularization of history, science, psychology, etc.; and biographies)	_____
"How-to" books (sex, gardening, cooking, etc.) or travel guides	_____
Technical reports/manuals/textbooks	_____
Poetry	_____
Children's books	_____
Religious/inspirational	_____
Translations	_____
Other	_____

Appendix B
Further Technical Considerations

In this appendix we present some technical material relating to the sample.

A Check on Response Bias

As noted in chapter 2, we conducted an indirect test of response bias comparing the distribution of responses in each of our three mailings—the first original questionnaire, the second sent to all nonrespondents, and the third miniquestionnaire mailed to a small subsample of nonresponding members of the guild. Since our study focuses on economic conditions, we mainly selected items that would detect any economic "success" or "failure" bias in our results.

The distribution of responses on nine items for each mailing is presented in table B.1. On every item the distribution of responses in the first and second mailing is very similar. The logic of our analysis thus suggests that the data do not reflect a notable response bias.

However, by comparison to the second mailing respondents, those forty-four authors responding to the third mailing were

- more productive, as measured by the number of books published;
- more likely to have been recently published;
- more likely to have been reviewed in the *New York Times* and have made a *New York Times* best-seller list before 1978;
- generally older and especially likely to be sixty-five or above.

Appendix B: Further Considerations

TABLE B.1. Distribution of Selected Variables by Mailing

Number of books published	First mailing	Second mailing	Third mailing
10+	26%	26%	41%
5–9	22%	26%	16%
3–4	21%	18%	20%
0–2	31%	31%	23%
Total	100% (1598)	101% (266)	100% (44)
Book published in 1977–79			
Yes	60%	56%	74%
No	40%	44%	26%
Total	100% (1727)	100% (511)	100% (42)
Book Reviewed in New York Times in 1978–1979			
Yes	23%	26%	21%
No	77%	74%	79%
Total	100% (1622)	100% (469)	100% (42)
Book reviewed in New York Times prior to 1978			
Yes	55%	55%	76%
No	45%	45%	24%
Total	100% (1575)	100% (445)	100% (42)
Age			
29 or less	2%	0%	0%
30–39	17%	15%	20%
40–49	25%	28%	14%
50–64	39%	38%	23%
65+	17%	20%	43%
Total	100% (1443)	101% (225)	100% (44)
Primary type of writing			
Genre fiction	13%	14%	11%
General adult fiction	20%	16%	14%
Academically oriented Nonfiction	12%	13%	5%
Adult nonfiction	26%	24%	32%
How-to books	6%	7%	9%
Technical reports, manuals, textbooks	3%	2%	5%
Poetry	2%	2%	2%
Children's books	15%	17%	18%
Religious inspirational	1%	1%	5%
Translations	0%	1%	0%
Other	2%	4%	0%
Total	100% (1660)	101% (488)	101% (44)
Book on New York Times best-seller list in 1978–79			
Yes	3%	3%	7%
No	97%	97%	93%
Total	100% (1651)	100% (479)	100 (42)
Book on New York Times best-seller list prior to 1978			
Yes	9%	10%	29%
No	91%	90%	71%
Total	100% (1696)	100% (462)	100% (41)

Appendix B: Further Considerations

TABLE B.1. *Continued*

Income related to books 1979			
$0–2,499	46%	46%	31%
$2,500–4,999	12%	15%	17%
$5,000–9,999	13%	11%	7%
$10,000–19,999	12%	12%	17%
$20,000–49,999	10%	7%	17%
$50,000–99,999	4%	7%	10%
$100,000+	3%	2%	2%
Total	100% (405)	100% (214)	101% (42)

These differences are all statistically significant at the conventional .05 level.

Although one should not infer too much because of the low response rate (29%) to the third mailing, the pattern of responses points to the possibility of some bias. At the same time, we should emphasize that the difference in book writing income—perhaps the most critical item for our purposes—is not statistically siginificant, even at the .20 level.

A Question of Weighting

Since we sampled from the lists of guild members and non-members at slightly different rates, the issue arose of whether we should weight the responses. (As stated in the text, a slightly higher proportion of guild members was included in the sample and therefore members and non-members had a slightly unequal chance of inclusion.) Theoretically, we could have weighted the responses of nonmembers and members so that they represented their proportional share of the population of authors.

However, this procedure was not practically possible. Since the proportional relation of the two lists to the population of authors remained unknown, a precise weighting factor could not be specified. Futhermore, since there is no evidence that the nonmembers were distinctly different from the members, weighting would have been superfluous. The absence of systmatic differences can be seen from results reported in table B.2. These data indicate:

- The difference in self-identification as a fulltime author was not statistically significant.[1]
- Nonmembers were only somewhat more likely than members to hold another paid job.

TABLE B.2. A Comparison of Members and Nonmembers: Selected Variables

		Members	Nonmembers	Significance at .05 level
Would you characterize your occupation as full-time freelance author or writer?	Yes	53% (960)	48% (171)	Not significant
	No	47% (865)	52% (189)	
Do you now hold a paid position besides freelance writing?	Yes	44% (801)	54% (194)	Significant
	No	56% (1011)	46% (167)	
Have any of your books been in the *New York Times Book Review* in 1978 or 1979?	Yes	23% (392)	28% (97)	Significant
	No	77% (1340)	72% (249)	
At any other time in the past?	Yes	55% (927)	52% (174)	Not significant
	No	45% (750)	(48% (158)	
Did you have a book on the *New York Times* best-seller lists at any time in 1978 or 1979?	Yes	3% (55)	4% (13)	Not significant
	No	97% (1707)	96% (341)	
At any other time in the past?	Yes	10% (172)	7% (24)	Not significant
	No	90% (1533)	93% (317)	
Genre: Genre fiction		13% (239)	10% (34)	⎫
General adult fiction		20% (354)	15% (54)	
Academically-oriented nonfiction		10% (183)	20% (70)	
Adult nonfiction		25% (446)	28% (100)	
How-to books		6% (110)	7% (23)	⎬ Significant
Technical reports		3% (57)	3% (11)	
Poetry		2% (33)	1% (4)	
Children's books		16% (282)	12% (43)	
Religious books		1% (22)	1% (2)	
Translations		0% (7)	0% (1)	
Other		2% (42)	3% (11)	⎭

		Members	Nonmembers
Total writing income for 1979	Median	$4,940 (1,615)	$4,650 (315)
Total personal income for 1979	Median	$26,780 (1,565)	$28,225 (310)
Total family income for 1979	Median	$37,800 (1,535)	$38,050 (307)

Appendix B: Further Considerations

- Nonmembers were a little more likely than members to have been reviewed in the *New York Times Book Review* in 1978–79, but there was not a statistically significant difference in the proportions having previous reviews. (A review in this publication may be considered an imperfect indicator of at least some critical recognition.)[2]
- In terms of making both recent and past *New York Times* best-seller lists, no significant difference occured between the members and nonmembers. (Making a best-seller list is an obvious indicator of substantial financial success in writing.)
- Members and nonmembers were distributed about equally throughout the country. This finding dispels the assumption in some circles that the guild is a particularly New York–oriented organization.
- Nonmembers were more likely than members to be academically oriented, nonfiction writers (10 percent versus 20 percent), but all other differences in writing genre were slight.
- The median 1979 figures for total personal income and total family income did not differ markedly.
- The median 1979 figures for writing income also did not differ substantially.

Across this considerable range of items, the members and nonmembers were remarkably similar. The few instances of a statistically significant difference reflected rather modest differences in everyday terms. In view of this similarity in responses, the issue of weighting factors receded in importance. We therefore simply aggregated the responses of the members and nonmembers without any weighing factor.

Appendix C

Results from Multiple Regression Analyses

In table C.1 the log of 1979 writing income and 1979 writing income is regressed on

1. Average number of hours a week writing;
2. Full-time/part-time status (1 = hold no other job; 0 = hold job);
3. Recency of publication (1 = 1977–1980; 2 = 1970–76; 3 = pre–1970);
4. Number of books;
5. Dummy variables for five genres of books—genre fiction, general adult fiction, adult nonfiction, and children's books.

We use the log transformation because of the skew in the distribution of income. Note that, because of missing observations for many variables, this regression equation is based on 1,425 cases, while there are 1,960 valid observations of writing income. Inspection of marginal distributions when categories of writing income are separately cross-classified with these factors suggests that the estimates are not likely to be appreciably affected by this reduction in the number of cases.

We view these equations as rough indicators of the relative magnitude of the independent relationships of these variables and writing income, as well as a summary device to indicate their collective contri-

TABLE C.1. Regression Analysis of 1979 Writing Income and Log of 1979 Writing Income by Selected Writing Career Factors

	Equation 1 Log of writing income			Equation 2 Writing income		
Independent variables	b	β	SE_b	b	β	SE_b
Intercept	8.12	0	.29	2793.8	0	6503.11
Hours/week writing	.04	.22	.00	513.3	.14	107.12
Full-time status	.31	.05	.16	7364.0	.06	3562.55
Recency of publication	−1.75	−.33	.13	−9073.4	−.08	2890.65
Number of books	.03	.13	.00	345.0	.07	131.63
Genre fiction	.31	.03	.25	22577.5	.12	5662.89
Adult fiction	.05	.00	.21	17582.4	.11	4728.10
Adult nonfiction	.26	.04	.19	3503.1	.02	4369.70
Children's books	−.06	.00	.24	13.1	.00	5362.49
Honor	.31	.07	.11	15370	.02	24249.49
R^2	.25			.08		

bution in accounting for variance. These equations should not be viewed as fully specified models of writing income.

We reiterate here, however, that models regressing 1979 writing income and the log of 1979 writing income on an extensive list of personal and social characteristics explained only 1 percent of the variance. Also, regression models incorporating human capital variables—job experience and education—explain no variance.

Appendix D

Classification of Awards and Publishing Houses

The following were designated major awards:

Academy of American Poets
American Academy and Institute of Arts and Letters
Bancroft Prize
Caldecott Medal (and Honor Books)
International Board on Books for Young People
Mystery Writers of America
Edgar Allen Poe Award (Edgar)
National Book Award (as of 1980 The American Book Awards, TABA)
National Book Critics Circle
National Medal for Literature
Newbery Medal (and Honor Books)
George Polk Award
Science Fiction Writers of America (Nebula Award)
Pulitzer Prize
World Science Fiction Convention (Hugo Award)
All other awards were designated minor awards. This classification follow the suggestion of our advisory board at the Authors Guild.

Appendix D: Awards and Houses

Publishing Houses

The following were designated major trade and mass market paperback houses:

Trade Book Houses
Atheneum
Atlantic Monthly Press/Little, Brown
Coward, McCann & Geoghegan
Delacorte Press
Dial Press
Doubleday
E.P. Dutton (Elsevier Dutton)
Farrar, Straus & Giroux
Harcourt Brace Jovanovich
Harper & Row
Holt, Rinehart & Winston
Houghton Mifflin
Alfred A. Knopf
Seymour Lawrence
Little, Brown
McGraw-Hill
Macmillan
William Morrow
Pantheon Books
C.P. Putnam's Sons (Putnam Publishing Group)
Random House
Charles Scribner's Sons
Simon & Schuster
Viking

Mass Market Paperback Houses
Avon Books
Ballantine Books
Bantam Books
Berkley
Dell
Fawcett (Crest, Gold Medal, Premier, Popular Library)
Jove
New American Library (NAL) (Signet, Mentor)
Pocket Books
Warner Books

Notes

1. INTRODUCTION

1. All but a few of the authors in the study had published at least one book, and these few others had published a number of articles in magazines.

2. There are several major sources on the history of authorship, and we have drawn heavily on these materials. The two most significant authorities, relied upon by a majority of scholars, are Alexandre Beljame's *Men of Letters and the English Public in the Eighteenth Century* (1948), and William Charvat's *Profession of Authorship in America, 1800–1870*, Matthew J. Bruccoli, ed. (1968). Among other sources, see Lewis Coser, *Men of Ideas* (1965), ch. 5, "The Profession of Letters in Eighteenth-Century England"; Victor Bonham-Carter, *Authors by Profession: Volume One* (1978), and *Authors by Profession: Volume Two, 1911–81* (1984); A. S. Collins, *The Profession of Letters* (1928), and *Authorship in the Days of Johnson* (1927); Ian Watt, *The Rise of the Novel* (1957); James Hepburn, *The Authors's Empty Purse and the Rise of the Literary Agent* (1968); George Woodcock, *The Incomparable Aphra* (1948); Edwin H. Miller, *The Professional Writer in Elizabethan England* (1959); Richard D. Altick, "The Sociology of Authorship: The Social Origins, Education, and Occupations of 1,100 British Writers, 1800–1935," *Bulletin of the New York Public Library* (June, 1962), 66 (6):389–404.

3. It is noteworthy that in both England and America, women were among the first truly professional writers of fiction. In Britain, Aphra Behn, celebrated perhaps more for her role as spy than as author, was one of the very first successful novelists, and her book, *Oroonoko*, has one of the first discussions of the so-called "material man" (Woodcock 1948). Similarly, Susannah Rowson, the author of *Charlotte's Temple*, which was first produced in England before she emigrated to the United States, and then reprinted here scores of times, can be said to be one of the first professional writers of fiction in this country.

4. In England as well, the development of lending libraries contributed to the rise of authorship as a profession. Those members of the literate middle class who could

not easily afford to purchase books could obtain them through lending libraries which began to be developed in the middle of the eighteenth century in England, the first one opening in London in 1740.

5. Fielding, who was a magistrate in the eighteenth century, and Trollope, who was a civil servant in the nineteenth, are two others among scores who relied upon other jobs to sustain their writing enterprises.

2. DESCRIPTION OF THE SURVEY OF AMERICAN AUTHORS

1. Some have suggested that the names of authors of works in *Books in Print* would be a more complete listing. However, many published authors who are currently active would be excluded because their books quickly went out of print as a result of poor sales. Such an exclusion would bias upward any estimates of authors' economic returns from writing. Also, there are practical difficulties: many of the authors listed in *Books in Print* are dead, and this source does not provide home addresses.

2. Decisions to reinvite authors are left to the discretion of the guild's clerical staff. Their decisions are based on their perception of the likelihood of gaining a member with a reinvitation. Generally, they let a few years go by before reinviting an author.

3. See Curtis Benjamin's "What Do Authors Really Earn?" *Publisher's Weekly*, February 19, 1982, for details of this criticism, and J. Cole, *Publisher's Weekly*, 1982, for a reply.

4. See the discussion "A Question of Weighting" in appendix B. There we indicate that on a series of critical items the guild members and nonmembers do not appreciably differ. In reporting the findings, we aggregated the responses of the members and nonmembers without any weighting factor.

5. We originally sent 5,145 questionnaires; of this total, 267 (5%) were undeliverable and 22 (.4%) were either foreign or dead.

6. A number of authors removed their identification numbers and others called us to ask how their confidentiality would be guarded.

7. Forty-six of the respondents could not be identified as members or nonmembers.

8. PEN is the second largest writers' organization in America; its membership overlaps to a considerable extent with that of the Authors Guild.

9. Our survey specified that "total income directly related to writing" included book royalties and subsidiary rights in addition to all unsalaried income derived from writing for magazines, newspapers, motion pictures, television, and radio. Income earned from salaried writing was excluded. The PEN survey does not specify the meaning of "income from writing," and therefore the cited figures may not be fully comparable. This survey was conducted by Philippe B. Perebimnossos. We thank him for making the results of the survey available to us.

10. Data were collected on the *New York Times* best-seller lists rather than others simply because they appeared to be the most widely known, not because they are necessarily the most accurate.

11. A reproduction of this miniquestionnaire appears in appendix A after the reproduction of the larger questionnaire.

12. For sources: Thomas F. Bradshaw, "An Examination of the Comparability of 1970 and 1980 Census Statistics on Artists," prepared for the Third International Conference on Cultural Economics and Planning, April 24–27, 1984 preprint; U.S. Bureau of the Census,

4. Income

Census of Population: 1970, *Subject Reports*, Final Report PC (2)-7A, Occupational Characteristics, table 1 and tabulations from the 1980 Census "EEO Special File" prepared by Data Use and Access Laboratories.

13. These difficulties were evident from the outset, and therefore intensive cooperation with an advisory board at the Authors Guild Foundation was essential. After we drafted a rough version of the questionnaire in response to the Foundation's general interests, the board members suggested revisions. The board members who advised us included Bruce Bliven, John Brooks, Peter Heggie, Sidney Offit, and Counsel Irwin Karp.

14. See particularly table 11.6, p. 173. See also Rossi and Lyall, 1976.

3. THE WRITING OCCUPATION

1. "Occupations and Careers," *International Encyclopedia of the Social Sciences*.

2. Our questionnaire asked the full-timers to specify the actual years (e.g., 1955–1961, 1972–1980) in which they were full-time writers, but, since there were so many incomplete or missing responses to this item, we could not systematically analyze the results. The conclusion here is based therefore on an inspection of the limited response to this item and should be treated with caution.

3. The figures in this paragraph on typical time allocations represent the median ratio of hours spent on other work to hours spent writing.

4. The other possible responses to this question were as follows: "Both complementary income and nonmonetary satisfaction"; "Derive most work-related satisfaction from this other work"; "Do not like writing full-time"; "Other: Specify."

4. INCOME

1. We should note further that the income schedule imposed a considerable burden on the respondents, even though we asked for estimated amounts rather than specific figures (which would have entailed going back to tax and other records). Not surprisingly, therefore, there is a considerable amount of missing data on a number of items. We asked the respondents to mark a "O" if they did not earn any money in a particular category, but many simply filled in the major aggregate totals (e.g., writing-related or total family) without providing any figures for the various subcategories. Others left some of the aggregate totals blank even though they completed the categories on which the totals are based.

In those cases—and only those cases—in which missing subcategory or total figures could be directly and unambiguously inferred, we coded in the appropriate figures. For example, if an author listed $5,000 for "total book income" and $5,000 for "total writing-related income," all of the intervening categories must necessarily be zero. However, with this procedure, not all blanks were treated as zero. For example, if a married author indicated a personal income of $15,000 but left the "spouse's income" and "total family income" blank, we treated "total family income" as missing information. In certain cases we might have a good sense that a particular blank line implied a zero value, but we still decided to treat it as a missing value. As a result, the various income figures are based on somewhat different numbers of cases. In the following analysis we therefore report the number of cases on which all summary measures are based.

2. The median is the value in an ordered set of values below and above which

there are an equal number of values. Since this measure is less affected by extreme high or low values than the arithmetic mean, it is generally preferred as a summary measure for income data.

3. This is an approximate figure, of course, since the work schedules of authors are frequently irregular, making estimations of the average number of hours spent at writing difficult to arrive at. We estimate the hourly income here by dividing each author's total income directly related to writing by the estimated average number of hours a week spent at writing (extended to a 50-week work year).

4. Bureau of Labor Statistics, "Union Wages and Benefits: Building Trades, July 3, 1978," bulletin 2039, 1979.

5. The typical case represents the median of the ratios of authors' book-related income to total writing-related income.

6. We caution against placing undue confidence in the exact figures relating to the ratio of royalty payments to total writing income because there were many missing cases. A number of authors reported total writing income but did not include a breakdown of their royalty payments. In all likelihood, the median ratio accurately suggests the overwhelming importance of royalty payments for most authors, but the precise degree of this importance is open to some question.

7. Writing income is represented in raw values and by three transformations, each of which is designed to reduce the effect of extreme cases in the overall distribution. Nevertheless, the size of the correlations is generally similar across all four measures of 1979 writing income.

8. See pp. 91–92 and appendix C.

9. Colleges and universities were categorized as "high prestige" (twenty-eight schools including the Ivy League) or "other." The coding scheme follows Kingston (1980) which is based on a prominent college admissions guidebook.

10. Of course, we can interpret these upper income figures in two ways. Either we note that there is only a 3 percent difference in the proportion of men and women authors who earned over $50,000 in 1979, or we note that almost one and a half times as many men as women are in this upper income group.

11. Obtaining precise estimates of the religious composition of the U.S. population is difficult since the census does not ask for the religious background of individuals. The source for the data reported here is *Statistical Abstract of the United States*, 1984, p. 58. These data are based upon church membership, and thus may be biased toward those religious groups who have more active members.

12. Since Catholic authors had the highest median writing incomes in 1979, their total will be used to compute all subsequent ratios used in this section.

13. If we compare mean writing incomes rather than medians, we find that both Jewish and Protestant authors earned roughly eight tenths of what Catholics earned.

14. To show the interactions between religious background and genre, we analyzed the ratios of median earnings (with Catholics again being the reference group) for the religious groups in major genres:

adult nonfiction: Jews, 1.28; Protestants, .82
academic nonfiction: Jews, 1.06; Protestants, 1.50
adult fiction: Jews, 1.08; Protestants, .58
genre fiction: Jews, .69; Protestants, .46
children's books: Jews, 1.37; Protestants, .50

15. To increase the number of cases to be analyzed, we also used age as a rough indicator of job experience. The results were similar.

4. Income

16. As quoted in Coser, Kadushin, and Powell 1982:317.

17. The major awards are listed in appendix D.

18. Of course, there is no clear-cut method of distinguishing major from less prominent publishing houses. Our classification was produced by our advisory board at the Authors Guild and is presented in appendix D.

19. We use the log transformation because of the skew in the distribution of income. These variables are much less able to explain variation (only 8 percent) in untransformed income. Commitments to genre and adult fiction independently affect untransformed income but not log of income.

20. The relevant literature is voluminous. For examples of sociological research see Jencks et al. (1979) and Featherman and Hauser (1978); in the human capital tradition within economics see Mincer (1974). Grandjean (1981) examines federal white-collar workers; Perrucci (1970) considers engineers; Cole and Cole (1973), among many others, analyze scientists; Rosenbaum (1979) considers private sector managers.

21. Jencks et al's (1979) findings, for example, indicate that status attainment models, incorporating the standard human capital variables relating to education and job experience, account for a tenth to a third of the variance in individual income. In Grandjean's analysis simple models incorporating only education and age were two to three times as powerful.

22. This figure also includes income from investments jointly held with a spouse.

23. The one exception to this generalization was the median level of 40 percent of personal income among the limited full-timers. It should be recognized, however, that about 40 percent of this group was over sixty-five, and therefore many relied primarily on these income sources. Indeed, they provided significant income only for older authors. The median for those sixty-five and over was $12,000; for those fifty to sixty-four, $2,000; and for all others, $0.

24. We include here the combined "total income directly related to writing" and "income from other freelance writing work" to give the broadest possible sense of the relative significance of writing activities. Since "income from other freelance writing" generally amounted to little, however, all ratios of the percentage contribution of "income directly related to writing" to personal income are only slightly less than those reported in this paragraph.

25. Total family income of single authors living alone is treated as the equivalent to their total personal income.

26. Census Bureau figures indicate that in 1979 81.4% of married men with the wife present were in the labor force; 49.4% of married women with husband present were in the labor force.

27. Census Bureau data suggest that these figures are not entirely in line with more general patterns: among married couple families in 1979 in which both spouses worked at least part of the time, the wife typically contributed 26.9% of family income. If they both worked full-time, full year, the figure was 34.7%. Thus the pattern within the families of female authors reflected more general patterns in the population, while the male authors contributed an unusually large proportion of family income.

28. This discussion of the role of "the spouse"—a man or woman formally married to someone of the opposite sex—does not take into account the increasing diversity of household arrangements in the lives of authors and others. In responding to the questionnaire, a number of homosexual authors emphasized this "conventionality" in forceful terms. To be sure, significant numbers of authors, both heterosexual and homosexual, share financial

burdens and resources with a partner on a relatively permanent basis. For these authors the financial contributions of their partners may be highly salient to their level of material comfort. Our reason of focusing on "conventional" marriages alone was simply that unmarried partnerships are so diverse in the ways incomes are merged that any related questionnaire item(s) would be misleading or overly cumbersome. By concentrating on married authors, we included the overwhelming number of those in relatively permanent partnerships and at the same time could assume a generally similar pattern of shared income.

29. In order to take into account the effect of inflation on income over a twenty-year period, we inflated the values of the 1957 income categories to 1978 dollars. Thus all comparisons are expressed in terms of 1978 purchasing power. The Implicit Price Deflator for Personal Consumption Expenditure in 1978 where 1957 = 100 is 217.00. We use 1978 data here because at the time of the analysis the deflator factor was not available for 1979.

30. The income data from the Society of Authors study reported by Findlater showed that full-time authors and those who classified themselves as "nearly" full-time had incomes well below £ 500 per year, or less than the minimum pay of a bus driver. Only about half earned as much as £ 500. From book rights and subsidiary rights in drama, television, translation, about one-sixth of the 1,587 authors who responded to the survey reported incomes greater than £ 1,050 a year, and two-thirds earned less than £ 312. Even allowing for inflation, these data suggest again, that authors in Britain as well as in the United States receive little compensation for their writing related publications (Hepburn 1968).

5. SOCIAL AND PROFESSIONAL CONNECTIONS AMONG AUTHORS

1. As quoted in Malcolm Cowley's (1954) "natural history" of the American writer.

2. As we will discuss, the authors with the most professional collaboration were overwhelmingly university teachers, a group which notably differs from the prevailing patterns of connections among authors in other respects as well.

3. Readers may want to refer back to chapter 3 to review the criteria used in creating this typology.

4. We have stressed here the role of the distinctive structural conditions of academic life in fostering the professional interaction of professor-authors rather than any personal characteristics. To reinforce this argument, we might add that professor-authors do not show some general disposition to talk writing, for they do not differ from other authors in their inclination to talk about their writing with nonauthors.

5. We use the same categorization of major and minor awards as discussed in "Critical Notice, Honorific Recognition, and Income" in chapter 4. See appendix D for details.

6. The general relationship between writing income (categorized into seven levels) and regularity of "writing talk" with fellow authors is not significant at the .05 level.

7. A recent best-seller is here defined as a book on one of the *New York Times* best seller lists, i.e., one of the top fifteen positions on the fiction or nonfiction hardcover lists or the mass or trade paper lists at any time in 1978 or 1979.

8. See appendix D, which classifies major and minor awards.

9. The correlation (Cramer's V) between honorific recognition and number of author friends (classified into four categories) is .14; the correlation between honorific recognition and frequency of social encounters is .09. It is indicative of the low patterning of social interaction among authors that none of the correlations between any of the inde-

6. Selected Portraits

pendent variables considered in this section and both frequency of contact and number of author friends exceeds .15.

10. The "academic exception" is discernible whether we define an academic as one who is a professor or as one who primarily writes academic nonfiction.

11. Again we must caution that the number of poets in our sample was small; inferences about the population of poets are necessarily tentative.

12. Our position follows the "production of culture" perspective which Peterson (1976) so convincingly champions. As he explains, this perspective focuses "on the processes by which elements of culture are fabricated in those milieux where symbol-system production is most self-consciously the center of activity" (p. 672).

13. Of course, many authors do thorough research, but few books for general audiences are at the "cutting edge" of a field. Popular histories, for instance, tend to distill existing published research, and no great need exists for personal contact with the specialists in the area.

14. In making this argument for using similar conceptual perspectives to study different cultural spheres, we repeat Diana Crane's (1974) general point in the chapter, "Toward a Sociology of Culture" in her influential book on the sociology of science, *Invisible Colleges: Diffusion of Knowledge in Scientific Communities*. See also Peterson (1976).

6. SELECTED PORTRAITS

1. The analysis involved in this collective portrait differs from that reported in chapter 4 about correlates of writing-related income. There we showed how various personal attributes affected the probability of earning particular levels of income. Here we show, for example, characteristics of the authors whose writing-related income was in the $0–$5,000 range; in effect, we alter the direction of percentaging the tables. The accuracy of the descriptions of these different groups depends, of course, on the adequacy of our sample. To the extent that there may have been systematic patterns to the nonresponses to the questionnaire, these group estimates may reflect those sample biases.

2. Recall that the median 1979 writing-related income was $4,775.

3. The responses of the rest were divided between "about equally satisfying" and "not sure."

4. As suggested by our previous discussion on the value of a "track record" (see chapter 4), these relatively financially successful writers were somewhat disproportionately productive as compared to their less financially successful counterparts.

5. Relative to the national distribution, a family income of $10,000–$20,000 corresponded approximately to the 30–60 percentiles.

6. Our estimates related to this group are especially open to question because of their low inclination to join the Authors Guild.

7. In terms of our five types of authors, the older writers were distributed as follows: Committed full-timers—36 percent; Limited full-timers—46 percent; Committed part-timers—3 percent; Significant part-timers—8 percent; and Marginal part-timers—7 percent.

8. An income edge accrued to the male authors within each of our five types.

APPENDIX B. FURTHER TECHNICAL CONSIDERATIONS

1. After computing chi square, we used the conventional .05 level of significance in this comparison and the others listed below.

2. We selected this publication because it is widely considered to be the most nationally prominent book review, not because its reviews are necessarily the most discerning or representative.

References

Altick, Richard D. 1962. "The Sociology of Authorship: The Social Origins, Education, and Occupations of 1,100 British Writers, 1800–1935." *Bulletin of the New York Public Library* (June), 66(6):389–404.
Baumol, William J. and William G. Bowen, 1966. *Performing Arts: The Economic Dilemma*. New York: The Twentieth Century Fund.
Becker, Gary. 1964. *Human Capital: A Theoretical and Empirical Analysis*. New York: Columbia University Press.
Beljame, Alexandre. 1948. *Men of Letters and the English Public in the Eighteenth Century*. London: Routledge and Kegan Paul.
Bellow, Saul. 1977. "Writers and Literature in American Society." In J. Ben-David and T. Clark, eds., *Culture and Its Creators*. Chicago: University of Chicago Press.
Benjamin, Curtis. 1982. "What Do Authors Really Earn?" *Publishers Weekly* (February 19), pp. 31–36.
Blau, Peter and Otis Dudley Duncan. 1967. *The American Occupational Structure*. New York: Wiley.
Blaug, Mark, ed. 1976. *The Economics of the Arts*. London: Martin Robertson.
Bowen, William G. and T. Aldrich Finegan. 1969. *The Economics of Labor Force Participation*. Princeton: Princeton University Press.
Bonham-Carter, Victor. 1978. *Authors by Profession: Volume One*. Los Altos, Cal.: Kaufmann.
Bonham-Carter, Victor. 1984. *Authors by Profession: Volume Two, 1911–81*. Los Altos, Cal.: Kaufmann.
Burt, Ronald S. 1982. *Toward a Structural Theory of Action*. New York: Academic Press.
Caplow, Theodore. 1954. *The Sociology of Work*. New York: McGraw-Hill.

References

Charvat, William. 1968. *The Profession of Authorship in America, 1800–1870.* Matthew J. Bruccoli, ed. Columbus: Ohio State University Press.

Cole, Jonathan R. 1978. *Fair Science: Women in the Scientific Community.* New York: Free Press.

Cole, Jonathan R. and Stephen Cole. 1973. *Social Stratification in Science.* Chicago: University of Chicago Press.

Collier, James Lincoln. 1981. "Can Authors Afford to Write Books?" *Publishers Weekly* (July 31), pp. 21–24.

Collins, A. S. 1927. *Authorship in the Days of Johnson.* London: Holden.

Collins, A. S. 1928. *The Profession of Letters.* London: Routledge and Kegan Paul.

Collins, Randall, 1979. *The Credential Society: A Historical Sociology of Education and Stratification.* New York: Academic Press.

Coser, Lewis. 1965. *Men of Ideas.* New York: Free Press.

Coser Lewis, Charles Kadushin, and Walter Powell. 1982. *Books: The Culture and Commerce of Publishing.* New York: Basic Books.

Cowley, Malcolm. 1954. *The Literary Situation.* New York: Viking.

Crane, Diana. 1972. *Invisible Colleges: Diffusion of Knowledge in Scientific Communities.* Chicago: University of Chicago Press.

Doeringer, Peter and Michael Piore. 1971. *Internal Labor Markets and Manpower Analysis.* Lexington, Mass.: Heath.

Duncan, O. D. 1968. "Inheritance of Poverty or Inheritance of Race?" In Daniel P. Moynihan, ed., *On Understanding Poverty,* pp. 85–110. New York: Basic Books.

O. D. Duncan, David Featherman, and Beverly Duncan. 1972. *Socioeconomic Background and Achievement.* New York: Seminar Press.

Featherman, David and Robert M. Hauser. 1978. *Opportunity and Change.* New York: Academic Press.

Form, William. 1968. "Occupations and Careers," In *International Encyclopedia of the Social Sciences,* 2:245–253. New York: Crowell, Collier, and Macmillan.

Grandjean, Burke. 1981. "History and Career in a Bureaucratic Labor Market." *American Journal of Sociology,* 86:1057–1092.

Granovetter, Mark. 1974. *Getting a Job.* Cambridge: Harvard University Press.

Greeley, Andrew M. 1976. *Ethnicity, Denomination, and Inequality.* Sage Research Papers in the Social Sciences. Beverly Hills: Sage.

Hagstrom, Warren O. 1976. "The Production of Culture in Science." *American Behavioral Scientist* (July/August), 19:753–768.

Hepburn, James. 1968. *The Author's Empty Purse and the Rise of the Literary Agent.* London: Oxford University Press.

Jencks, Christopher et al. 1979. *Who Gets Ahead? The Determinants of Economic Success in America.* New York: Basic Books.

Johnstone, John W. C., Edward Slowski, and William Bowman. 1976. *The News People: A Sociological Portrait of American Journalists and Their Work.* Urbana: University of Illinois Press.

Kadushin, Charles. 1974. *The American Intellectual Elite.* Boston: Little, Brown.

Kadushin, Charles. 1976. "Networks and Circles in the Production of Culture." *American Behavioral Scientist* (July-August), 19:769–784.

References

Kershaw, David and Jerilyn Fair. 1976. *New Jersey Income-Maintenance Experiment, Volume I: Operations Surveys and Administration.* New York: Academic Press.

Lord, William J., Jr. 1962. *How Authors Make a Living: An Analysis of Free Lance Writers' Incomes 1953–1957.* New York: Scarecrow Press.

Merton, Robert K. 1973. *The Sociology of Science.* Chicago: University of Chicago Press.

Miller, Edwin H. 1959. *The Professional Writer in Elizabethan England.* Cambridge: Harvard University Press.

Mincer, J. 1974. *Schooling, Experience, and Earnings.* New York: Columbia University Press.

Perucci, C. 1970. "Minority Status and the Pursuit of Professional Careers: Women in Science and Engineering." *Social Forces,* 49:245–259.

Peterson, Richard. 1976. "The Production of Culture: A Prolegomenon." *American Behavioral Scientist* (July-August), 19:669–684.

Price, D. J. de Solla. 1963. *Big Science, Little Science.* New York: Columbia University Press.

Reiss, A. et al. 1961. *Occupations and Social Status.* New York: Free Press.

Rogers, A. et al. 1970. "The Batignolles Group: Creators of Impressionism." In M. Albrecht, J. Barnett, and M. Griff, eds., *The Sociology of Arts and Leisure,* pp. 194–220. New York: Praeger.

Rosenbaum, J. 1979. "Organizational Career Mobility: Promotion Chances in a Corporation During Periods of Growth and Contraction." *American Journal of Sociology,* 85:21–48.

Rosenberg, B. and N. E. Fliegel. 1965. *The Vanguard Artist.* Chicago: Quadrangle Books.

Rosenberg, Harold. 1970. "The Art Establishment." In M. Albrecht, J. Barnett, and M. Griff, eds., *The Sociology of Arts and Leisure,* pp. 388–395. New York: Praeger.

Rossi, Peter and Katharine Lyall. 1976. *Reforming Public Welfare: A Critique of the Negative Income Tax Experiment.* New York: Russell Sage.

Santos, F. P. 1976. "Risk, Uncertainty, and the Performing Artist." In Mark Blaug, ed., *The Economics of the Arts,* pp. 243–259. London: Martin Robertson.

Sullivan, D., D. H. White, and E. J. Barboni. 1977. "Co-Citation Analyses of Science: An Evaluation." *Social Studies of Science* (May), 7:223–241.

Treiman, Donald J. 1977. *Occupational Prestige in Comparative Perspective.* New York: Academic Press.

Watt, Ian. 1957. *The Rise of the Novel.* Berkeley and Los Angeles: University of California Press.

White, Harrison and C. White. 1965. *Canvases and Careers.* New York: Wiley.

Wilson, R. N. 1958. *Man Made Plain.* Cleveland: Howard Allen.

Woodcock, George. 1948. *The Incomparable Aphra.* London and New York: T. V. Boardman.

Zuckerman, Harriet. 1977. *The Scientific Elite: Nobel Laureates in the United States.* New York: Free Press.

Name Index

Baumol, William, 96
Becker, Gary, 81
Beljame, Alexandre, 9, 12, 15
Bellow, Saul, 109, 110
Benchley, Robert, 1, 163
Benjamin, Curtis, 27–29
Blaug, Mark, 96
Bonham-Carter, Victor, 9, 10, 11, 15, 16
Bowen, William, 96

Caplow, Theodore, 19
Charvat, William, 16
Cole, Jonathan, 140, 197
Cole, Stephen, 140, 197
Collier, James, 58–59
Collins, A. S., 9, 10, 14
Cooper, James Fenimore, 16
Coser, Lewis, 10, 11, 13, 14, 15, 20, 21, 73, 97, 144, 147, 197
Cowley, Malcolm, 3, 109, 198
Crane, Diana, 140, 199

Dryden, John, 10, 15

Emerson, Ralph, 18

Grandjean, Burke, 96, 197

Hagstrom, Warren, 140
Hawthorne, Nathaniel, 17, 18

Hemingway, Ernest, 109, 123
Hepburn, James, 31, 198

Johnson, Samuel, 14, 165

Kadushin, Charles, 20, 21, 73, 97, 142, 144, 145, 147, 197

Lord, William, 31, 105, 106, 107

Melville, Herman, 18
Merton, Robert K., 41, 140
Milton, John, 10
Mincer, Jacob, 84

Peterson, Richard, 199
Pope, Alexander, 10, 11, 15
Powell, Walter, 20, 21, 73, 97, 144, 147, 197
Price, D. J. de Solla, 140, 143

Rosenberg, B., 141, 146

Santos, Fredricka, 93–94, 98

Thoreau, Henry David, 18

Watt, Ian, 9, 13, 14
White, Harrison, 141, 146
Wilson, R. N., 116, 136

Zuckerman, Harriet, 140

Subject Index

Academic authors: attitudes about career, 50; influence of other authors, 135–36; prevalence of, 48; professional interaction, 113–14, 116; social interaction, 124
Advance subscriptions, 14
Age: effects on other discussions about writing, 120–21; effects on professional interaction, 119; older authors, 157–58; young authors, 156–57
Articles and scripts: income from, 60; relation to definition of authors, 4
Artists, 141, 145, 146
Author: definition of, 2–4, 19–20, 24; economic condition in eighteenth-century England, 9; economic condition in nineteenth-century America, 17–19; history of profession, 9–19; origins in England, 9; public opinion of, 2; stereotypes of, 1; typology of, 44–46
Authors Guild, ix, x, 25, 26, 195; advisory board, 195; membership list, 25

Best-selling authors, 154–56; professional connections of, 115; representative sampling of, 33–34

Census (U.S.): characteristics of authors, 35–37; definition of, 24; incomes of other occupations, 99

Children's books (authors): income of, 84, 86; prevalence of, 84; professional interaction, 118; social interaction, 118
Connections (among authors): by comparison to artists, 141, 146; by comparison to Europe, 139; by comparison to intellectuals, 145–46; by comparison to scientists, 139–41; role of "external economy", 142–47; theoretical explanation of, 142–47; *see also* Influence of other authors; Professional connections; Social connections
Commission publishing, 15
Copyrights, sale of, 15
Culture, *see* Sociology of culture

Education: effects on income, 72–73; effects of college prestige, 72–73
England: authors' incomes in, 198; connections among authors, 110, 139; development of profession, 9–16
External economy, 142–45

Family background: effects on income, 70, 71–72; effects on professional interaction, 119; effects on social interaction, 127
Family income: changes in, 107; contribution of spouse, 104–5; contribution of writing income, 104; definition of, 102; summary measures, 102–4

Fiction (authors of): income of, 84, 86; influence patterns among, 136; prevalence of, 84; professional interaction, 116
Full-time authors 45, 46–48; career movement, 46–47; family income, 102, 104; hours worked, 43; other work, 47–48; personal income, 102; professional interaction, 113; social connections, 124; types of, 45

Genre (of books): relation to writing income, 82–86, 92; variations in discussions of writing, 120; variations in influence patterns, 136; variations in professional connections, 115–18; variations in social connections
Grub Street, 11, 12

Honorific recognition: and author friends, 125; and fequency of professional connections; and frequency of social connections; and income, 88–90, 92
Hours worked, 42–43; and income, 64–70, 91; men and women, 76
Human capital theory, 81, 82, 92, 96, 98

Income, see Family Income; Income Changes; Income Fluctuations; Personal Income; Writing Income
Income Changes: comparison with earlier data, 105–7
Income Fluctuations, 60–64
Influence of other authors, 133–36; effects of personal connections, 134
Internal labor markets, 95, 96
Intellectuals; 145–46
Investment income, 101

Low-income authors, 150–52

Modestly successful authors, 152–54

Networks: see influence patterns; Professional connections; Social Connections
New York (authors): connections among, 118–19, 125–27, 139; discussions with others, 120; income of, 73–74; prevalence of, 36

New York Times: best-seller lists and response bias, 33–34; importance of reviews in, 86, 88
Nonfiction (authors of): income of, 84, 86; influence patterns among, 136; prevalence of, 84; professional interaction, 116

Other jobs (of authors): attitudes toward, 50–52; effects on writing, 52–53; income from, 99–101; irregular, writing related jobs, 47; types, 48–49

Part-time authors, 45–46; attitudes toward other jobs, 50–53; attitudes toward writing, 50–53; effects of other jobs on writing, 52–53; family income, 102, 104; hours worked, 43; nonwriting work hours, 49–50; other occupations, 48–49; personal income, 102; professional connections, 113; social connections, 124; types of, 45–46; why other jobs, 51; writing income, 64–65
PEN survey of authors: income data, 32; response, 31
Personal income: comparison with other occupations, 99; investments, pensions and Social Security, 101–2; proportional contribution of writing income, 120; salaries from other jobs, 99–101; summary measures, 99
Poetry (authors of): connections among poets, 116; influence patterns among, 136; motivation for, 93
Profession (of authors): historical development of in England, 9–16; uncertain nature of, 19–20, 42; in the United States, 16–19
Professional connections (among authors): discussions with other authors, 111–13; discussions with others, 119–21; in Europe, 110; general lack of connections, 121–23; *relation to* genre, 116–18, to occupational commitment, 113, to social connections, 111, 128–33, to success, 115, to writing activity, 114–15
Publishing houses: categorization of, 192; effects on writing income, 90–91

Race (of authors): effects on income, 74
Religious background (of authors): effects on

Subject Index

income, 76–80
Royalty payments, 59

Scientists, 72, 75, 78, 114, 140–41, 142–45
Sexual differences: in discussions with others, 121; in genre, 76; in income, 75–76; in professional connections, 119; in social connections, 127; in spouse's role, 105; *see also* Women authors
Social connections (among authors): in Europe, 110; extent, 123–26; number of author friends, 124; *relation to* genre, 125, to occupational commitment, 124, to professional connections, 111, 128–33, to success, 124–25
Sociology of culture: connections among different kinds of "culture producers", 139–42; structural differences among authors, 136–38; theoretical explanation of connections among producers, 142–46
Sociology of occupations, 19; distinctiveness of authors, 81–82, 92–95; explanations of intraoccupational success, 95–99
Spouses (of authors), 104–5, 164
Subscription as form of payment, 15
Subsidiary rights, 59–60
Survey: population parameters, 23–25; questionnaire design, 37–39; respone, 30–31; response bias checks, 32–35, 183–85; sample size, 29; sampling frames, 25–29

Typology of authors, 44; *relation of types* to discussion with others, 120, to family income, 102, to influence patterns, 135, to personal income, 102, to writing income, 66, 74–76

Women authors, 74–76, 158–62; *see also* Sexual differences
Work commitment: hours worked, 42–43; relation to income, 64–70; self-identification, 42–43
Writing income: changes in, 106–7; contribution to family income, 104; to personal income, 102; definition, 56–57; fluctuations, 60–64; *relation* to college prestige, 72, to critical notice, 86–90, to education, 72–73, *to* family background, 71–72, to genre, 82–86, to geographical location, 73–74, to honorific recognition, 86–90, to job experience, 81, to occupational commitment, 64–70, to personal characteristics, 71–81, to publication history, 82, to publishing house, 91, to race, 74, to religious background, 76–80, to sex, 74–76; sources of, 59–60; summary measures of, 57–58

Young authors, 156–57